LONDON

THE STORY OF A GREAT CITY

PREVIOUS PAGE A Roman plaque from AD300–350, the earliest evidence we have that the city was known as Londinium; it was found buried in a temple courtyard in Southwark.

OPPOSITE A thirteenth-century circular red wax seal showing St Paul, Patron Saint of London, with a panorama of the city beneath his feet.

For Rosie Cooper

Text © Jerry White 2010
Design © Carlton Books Ltd 2010

First published in 2010 by Andre Deutsch
An imprint of the Carlton Publishing Group
20 Mortimer Street, London W1T 3JW

A CIP catalogue record for this book is available from the British Library.

ISBN: 978 0 233 00285 9

Publishing Manager: Penny Craig
Designer: Lucy Coley
Picture Research: Sean Waterman and Stephen Behan
Production: Rachel Burgess

Printed in China

LONDON

THE STORY OF A GREAT CITY

JERRY WHITE

MUSEUM
OF LONDON

ANDRE
DEUTSCH

CONTENTS

LEFT A City of London police call post from the 1930s. Any member of the public needing assistance could open the door, lift the receiver and speak directly to the police station.

PREFACE

London is now some two-thousand years old, and for the last thousand at least it has been one of the greatest cities on earth. For many centuries it was the biggest city in the western hemisphere, not just in terms of the ground it covered but in the vast numbers who chose to live there. It was the world's chief port, the capital of the world's biggest empire, the heart which pumped money into every country's coffers, the major producer of fine commodities for discerning purchasers everywhere, a city where startling riches and starving poverty lived side by side, and where the world's communities, whether fleeing persecution or seeking a better life, found a congenial and reasonably tolerant home.

These giant achievements were not won without a struggle. No city can lay claim to a more dramatic history than London. Engulfed in calamities that seemed to mark its end – fire, plague, riot, civil war, mass bombing – from each crisis it has emerged stronger than ever. And its cultural life, and the long heritage that underpins it, has made London one of the most visited and best-loved places on earth. Now it is one of just a handful of "World Cities" that belong less to a nation than to the global community as a whole.

In telling these stories, this book relies as much on its illustrations as on its text. I have been fortunate indeed in being able to draw on the fabulous resources of the Museum of London, one of the world's great city museums. Its uniquely rich collections illuminate the whole of London's history through objects, artefacts, maps, documents, paintings and photographs, and its long tradition as an educator of generations of Londoners has greatly aided the choice and presentation of material.

In particular, the Museum has been intimately concerned in the choice of the facsimiles reproduced here. These high-quality reproductions bring home to us the look and feel of documents and other objects that helped Londoners understand, explain and enjoy their city.

Through this combination of text, illustrations and facsimiles I hope that we have brought the history of this unique city vividly alive once more.

Jerry White
April 2010

ABOVE AND RIGHT Stone blocks from Guildhall Chapel commemorating the mayoralties of Henry Frowyk (mercer, 1435–36 and 1444–45) and Thomas Knollys (or Knolles) (grocer, 1399–1400 and 1410–11).

NEXT PAGE Twenty-first century London at night, the illuminated pedestrian walkways of Hungerford Railway Bridge in the foreground, the London Eye on the South Bank, and Westminster and the Houses of Parliament across the Thames.

London and Westminster

The ancient heart of London, the part that most of the world knows, is in fact not one city but two. Something like a thousand years separates their real beginnings. Everything in London starts with the Romans and their city, Londinium, came first. It was founded around the year AD 48, planted on gravel and clay where no continuous human settlement had been before. The new city was central to the new northern province of Britannia and soon became its greatest centre of trade, wealth and power. Around 200–225, its defences were strengthened with giant walls on three sides, the river Thames providing safety from the south until this too was walled around 300. Behind these fortifications, London remained safe until the Roman grip weakened and then relaxed altogether around 410.

In the troubled times that followed the end of the Roman province, London declined and was at least partly abandoned. The Anglo-Saxon invaders who then followed in the wake of Roman withdrawal eventually settled in or around the city. A new commercial district was established beyond the western walls, but was abandoned in the face of attacks by Viking raiders (predominantly Danish) in the ninth century, in favour of the old walled city, now called Lundenburg. It was the final defeat of the Danes and the re-establishment of an Anglo-Saxon king, Edward the Confessor, in 1042 that changed the fortunes of London forever. It was Edward who moved his court two and a half kilometres (a mile and a half) west of the old city to what would eventually become the City of Westminster; and it was Edward who also laid the foundations of a great church there that became Westminster Abbey.

This was the defining moment in the creation of London's great duality: the commercial trading and industrial city in the east on the old footprint of Roman Londinium (which would become the City of London); the city of court, church and state in a new settlement in the Anglo-Saxon west. This bi-polar arrangement would define the nature of London for a thousand years to come.

WESTMINSTER ABBEY, St MARGARET'S CHURCH & the NEW SQUARE *FROM PARLIAMENT STREET.*

Published 20th July 1822, by R.H.LAURIE N°.53.Fleet Street.London.

A year after the consecration of Edward's new Abbey in 1065, the Norman invasion gave England and London new rulers. The Normans consolidated London's dual status. They provided new fortifications for London and its river with a castle at the south-east corner of the Roman wall: William the Conqueror's Tower of London was a building of imposing strength and grandeur. It was followed, in the west of the old city, by a Norman St Paul's Cathedral on the site of a Saxon predecessor that burned down in 1087. And further west still, the king's palace was extended with one of the greatest of all surviving early medieval structures, Westminster Hall.

For the next 500 years, the development of London was dominated by the cementing together of London and Westminster. The main connection was the river and a single road, the old line of Fleet Street and the north bank of the Thames called the Strand. By the time of Elizabeth I (1558–1603), the riverfront was continuously developed, with a new royal palace at Whitehall and great aristocratic mansions with ornamental gardens running down to the riverside. The prevailing winds drove the smoke and stench of the City of London away from Westminster's royal residents. That, and the proximity to the most powerful in the land, would make Westminster an attractive prospect for the rich to plant their houses in the generations to come.

The old city did not stand still. Building spilled beyond the Roman walls in all directions. The poorest, and those involved in riverside trades, settled in the east; the middling sort moved towards the hills in the north; and the best-off got as close to the court as they could in the west (which would become known in time as the West End). Under the Tudors, the port extended more confidently downriver from its traditional site in the old

ABOVE Westminster Abbey in the summer of 1822, with Nicholas Hawksmoor's twin Gothic towers at the west end just 77 years old, and St Margaret's church in the foreground.

LEFT An imaginative reconstruction of Roman London, AD 250, looking from the north-west. Beyond the walls, the River Fleet forms a marshy estuary on the right. The square building north of London Bridge is the Basilica, and nearest us is the great fort at Cripplegate.

THE TOWER OF LONDON

Begun in the late 1070s with the White Tower, and added to over the next three centuries, this is London's medieval castle, protecting the city at the point most vulnerable to an invasion from the sea. Its dense fortifications have made it an ideal prison over the centuries, especially for those considered enemies of the state. Beheadings of "traitors" and "heretics" took place before great crowds on Tower Hill into the eighteenth century, and even in the Second World War it was used briefly to hold the high-ranking Nazi, Rudolf Hess. The Tower remains one of London's great tourist attractions, housing the Crown Jewels and the Royal Armouries. The illustration shows the Tower in 1651.

BELOW The Rhinebeck Panorama shows the Thames around 1806, alive with shipping near the Tower. London Bridge is in the foreground, Blackfriars Bridge beyond it, and Westminster Bridge on the left after the great bend of the river.

Roman heart. And under the Stuarts in the seventeenth century, London thickened out and consolidated in all directions. It did so especially around Westminster. It was the period between 1670 and the end of the eighteenth century that saw the court end of the town acquire the elegant squares (St James's, Hanover, Berkeley, Grosvenor, Cavendish) and the beginnings of the luxurious shopping streets (Piccadilly, Bond Street, Savile Row) that define the West End of London to this day.

The duality of these two ancient cities is readily apparent still. The West End has been vastly expanded in the last 150 years, with Oxford Street the premier shopping street of all England. The City of London has maintained an entirely distinctive identity as one of the great financial trading districts of the world. Their differences are revealed not just at street level but in their skylines. They remain the twin ventricles at the heart of London. But from these two beginnings, London would become so much more.
See also facsimile item 1 in envelope 1, opposite page 20.

LEFT The twenty-first century skyline looking to the south-west from St Paul's; the Palace of Westminster is prominent in the centre and Big Ben is to the right, encircled by the London Eye.

City of Suburbs

IN Roman London, the Thames was some five times wider at high tide than it is today and a bridge was essential to connect London with the ports along the English Channel. By around the year 90 some reasonably permanent wooden structure was in place. At the southern end of the bridge a later fortification – known as the south-wark – protected it from attack. Between 1176 and 1205, Peter de Colechurch, a priest, oversaw the building of the first London Bridge to be made of stone: he died four years before its completion in 1209. The bridge outlasted him by over 600 years. Its roadway was cluttered with houses on both sides until the 1750s, while its nineteen arches caused waterfalls of such frightening depth from one side of the bridge to the other that only the most daring watermen would attempt the passage. It was this great bridge, replaced in 1831 and again in 1972, that established the market town of Southwark as the commercial gateway to London from the south.

BELOW The Great Fire of London as seen from a boat in the vicinity of Tower Wharf. Backlit by flames, you can see Old London Bridge, the churches of St Dunstan-in-the-West and St Bride's, All Hallows the Great, Old St Paul's, St Magnus the Martyr, St Lawrence Pountney, St Mary-le-Bow and St Dunstan-in-the East and the Tower of London on the right.

OPPOSITE Two proposed plans for the reconstruction of London after the Great Fire. The top design by John Evelyn consists of 12 interconnecting squares and piazzas. The Royal Exchange is re-sited where Cannon Street Station now is; a straight west-to-east thoroughfare cuts its way from Temple Bar to "King Charles Gate" south of Aldgate. The bottom design by Sir Christopher Wren shows broad boulevards and open squares replacing the warren of alleys and byways. Neither plan was ever executed.

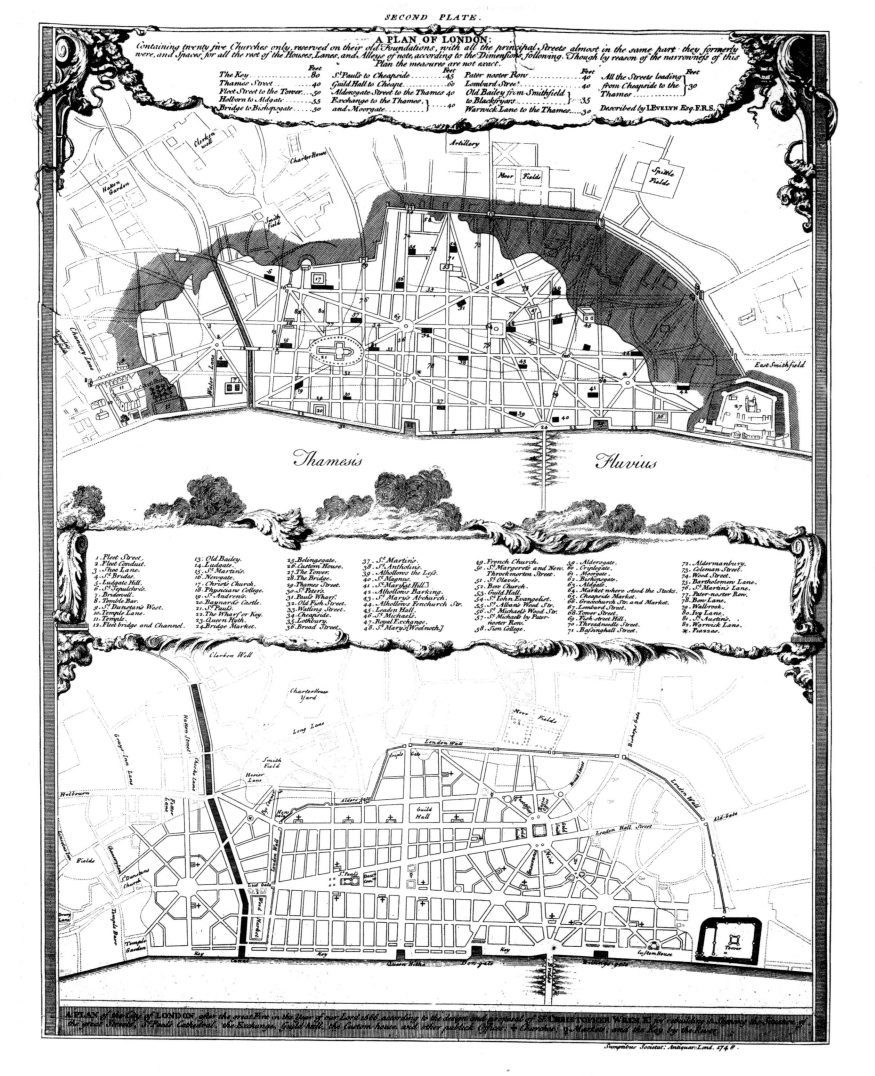

A PLAN OF LONDON:

Containing twenty five Churches only, reserved on their old Foundations, with all the principal Streets almost in the same part they formerly were, and Spaces for all the rest of the Houses, Lanes, and Alleys of note, according to the Dimensions following. Though by reason of the narrowness of this Plan the measures are not exact.

	Feet		Feet		Feet		Feet
The Key.	80	St Paul's to Cheapside.	45	Pater noster Row	40	All the Streets leading	
Thames Street	40	Guild Hall to Cheape.	60	Lombard Stree'.	40	from Cheapside to the	30
Fleet Street to the Tower	50	Aldersgate Street to the Thames	40	Old Bailey from Smithfield		Thames	
Holborn to Aldgate	55	Exchange to the Thames	} 40	to Blackfryars	} 35		
Bridge to Bishopsgate	50	and Moorgate.		Warnick Lane to the Thames	30	Described by J. Evelyn Esq. F.R.S.	

Clerken well

Charter House

Hatton Garden

Smith Field

Artillery

Moor Field

Spittle Fields

Chancery Lane

Thamesis

Fluvius

East Smithfield

1. Fleet Street.	13. Old Bailey.	25. Belingsgate.	37. St Martin's.	49. French Church.	59. Aldersgate.	72. Aldermanbury.
2. Fleet Conduit.	14. Ludgate.	26. Custom House.	38. St Antholin's.	50. St Margaret's and New.	60. Criplegate.	73. Coleman Street.
3. Shoe Lane.	15. St Martin's.	27. The Tower.	39. Alhollows the Less.	Throckmorton Street.	61. Moorgate.	74. Wood Street.
4. St Brides.	16. Newgate.	28. The Bridge.	40. St Olaves.	51. St Magnus.	62. Bishopsgate.	75. Bartholomew Lane.
5. Ludgate Hill.	17. Christ's Church.	29. Thames Street.	41. St Mary at Hill.	52. Bow Church.	63. Aldgate.	76. St Martins Lane.
6. St Sepulchre's.	18. Physicians College.	30. St Peter's.	42. Alhollows Barking.	53. Guild Hall.	64. Market where stood the Stocks.	77. Pater-noster Row.
7. Bridewell.	19. St Andrew's.	31. Pauls Wharf.	43. St Marys Abchurch.	54. St John Evangelist.	65. Cheapside Market.	78. Bow Lane.
8. Temble Bar.	20. Baynard's Castle.	32. Old Fish Street.	44. Alhollows Fenchurch Str.	55. St Alban's Wood Str.	66. Gracechurch Str. and Market.	79. Wallbrook.
9. St Dunstan's West.	21. St Pauls.	33. Watling Street.	45. Leaden Hall.	56. St Michaels Wood Str.	67. Lombard Street.	80. Ivy Lane.
10. Temple Lane.	22. The Wharf or Key.	34. Cheapside.	46. St Michaels.	57. St Michaels by Pater-	68. Tower Street.	81. St Austin's.
11. Temple.	23. Queen Hyth.	35. Lothbury.	47. Royal Exchange.	noster Row.	69. Fish street Hill.	82. Warnick Lane.
12. Fleet bridge and Channel.	24. Bridge Market.	36. Bread Street.	48. St Marys [Woolnoth]	58. Sion College.	70. Threadneedle Street.	*. Piazzas.
					71. Bassinghall Street.	

Clerken Well

Charterhouse Yard

Long Lane

Smith Field

Hosier Lane

Moor Fields

London Wall

Cripple Gate

Holborn

Guild Hall

Bishops Gate

London Wall

Aldersgate

Leaden Hall Street

Ald-Gate

Fields

St Dunstans Church

St Pauls

Lud Gate

Drury Lane

Temple Bar

Temple Garden

Key

Key

Queen Hithe

Downgate

Key

Custom House

Tower

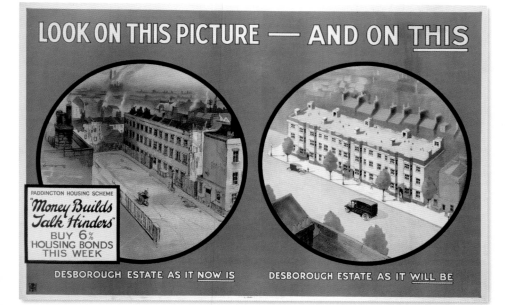

Covent Garden Piazza and Market around 1730, showing market stalls with their vendors and some prosperous-looking customers. At night, the Piazza was the hub of London prostitution, but here – in daylight – decorum temporarily reigns.

LEFT This poster from 1920 shows a "before and after" image of the new housing that was planned to replace the existing slums of the Desborough Estate in Paddington, west London. The London County Council encouraged the public to buy 6% Housing Bonds that would help to make modern housing a reality.

BELOW Bedford Park, in Chiswick, west London, was one of the first garden suburbs, built in the late nineteenth century. The houses and public spaces were designed by the leading architects of the day. This lithograph shows Bath Road, looking east. The area is still popular – and expensive – today.

But Southwark was not London. It maintained its own identity and traditions and claims by the City of London to govern it would be bitterly contested for centuries. "South London" was not an idea which would be given a name until the early nineteenth century.

If Southwark was a suburb in waiting, developments to the north and north-west of the Roman city would properly claim a suburban and dependent status. It was in the seventeenth century in particular that the ancient settlement of Holborn became attached to London. Within it, St Giles was a poor district from the outset, while Lincoln's Inn Fields was a giant square laid out for prosperous tenants between 1638 and 1657. Covent Garden, a rare instance of early London town planning, developed around the same time on land owned by the Earls of Bedford.

Covent Garden was not yet complete when one of the greatest disasters ever to befall London struck in the early morning of Sunday September 2, 1666 at Farynor's bakery, Pudding Lane. Fire had always been a threat to this largely wood-built city, but there had never been anything to match the Great Fire of London. Fanned by a strong wind, it raged for four days. It was said to have destroyed over 13,000 houses, 87 churches and more than 60 public buildings, including four prisons. Three-quarters of the City within the walls and a good deal more at the edges was wiped from the earth.

The City was largely rebuilt within around 20 years, though the new St Paul's Cathedral, Sir Christopher Wren's masterpiece, would not finally be completed until 1710. Surprisingly, many rebuilt City houses did not easily find tenants, a phenomenon explained by the huge push which the Great Fire gave to the expansion of London. Many Fire victims, the better-off among them, chose to settle in the new suburbs. It was in these post-Fire years that Covent Garden became a prominent retail district, colonized by former City tradesmen. And entirely new developments – Soho, Seven Dials, Leicester Square – were established to meet the demand. By 1700, London was the biggest city in the western world, home to around half a million people.

For the next 250 years, the growth of London would hardly pause for breath. It nearly all took place on the north side of the Thames until two vigorous periods of bridge-building encouraged growth to the south of the river. Westminster Bridge connected London to Lambeth from 1750 and soon after Blackfriars Bridge helped Southwark grow west of its ancient high street. After the Napoleonic Wars, Vauxhall Bridge (1816), Waterloo Bridge (1817) and Southwark Bridge (1819) began to make South London a genuine reality.

The nineteenth century witnessed London moving so fast outwards that farms, fields and villages in every direction were buried under brick and mortar in what seemed like the twinkling of an eye. The city had housed around a million people in 1800. A century later it would be home to over 6,580,000. Nor did development stop there. In the first 40 years of the twentieth century London's built-up area would double in size again. By 1939, it was 55 kilometres (34 miles) across, its outer districts covered with suburban semi-detached houses. And its population reached 8,615,000 – its historic high-point, never surpassed since.

It was the Green Belt (a zone around the city within which further development was not permitted, put in place from the 1930s to the 1950s) that eventually brought a halt to the growth of London. Fortunately so, for where might it all have ended? And this huge expansion left Londoners with one enduring problem: how to get around their monster city.

See also facsimile item 2 in envelope 1, opposite page 20.

Getting Around

FOR over 1,800 years, most Londoners got around their city on foot. London was then still walkable and Shanks's pony the cheapest form of locomotion. Only the well-off rode horses, had carriages or were carried in chairs. Even goods were often moved on porters' backs – there were special stones on the pavements on which they could rest their loads. Those who took to carriages suffered dislocating jolts from the uneven road surfaces that plagued the city well into the 1760s.

The earliest forms of public transport began on the river. While London had just one hugely congested bridge, a lot of this was cross-river traffic. Being rowed upriver from the City to Westminster and Whitehall – leaving aside the hazards of London Bridge which many travellers avoided by landing either side of it – was the quickest and most comfortable way of getting around. Fares were regulated from 1514 and it was said in the time of Elizabeth that there were 40,000 earning their living on the Thames. Watermen were known for their truculent tempers, foul language and reckless practical joking against other river users, especially those rowing for pleasure. But the new bridges undermined their livelihoods and by the middle of the nineteenth century they were few and far between.

RIGHT A South London horse-drawn tram, photographed for a lantern slide around 1890. Trams could move more passengers using less horse-power, and so more cheaply, than horse buses.

BELOW LEFT The world's first underground railway in the world, the Metropolitan Railway, opened in January 1863. This third-class ticket for a short stage, costing just a penny, is from the railway's early years.

BELOW RIGHT From the early 1700s, local Turnpike Trusts took over responsibility for repairing the main roads to and from London. Road users on horseback or in coaches, carriages and wagons had to pay a toll at turnpikes and were given a ticket, like this one for the Marylebone & Finchley Roads trust.

GOING UNDERGROUND

The first great extension of the underground was in the 1860s, from Paddington through Kensington, then along the Victoria Embankment to Blackfriars in the City, now part of the District and Circle lines. Tunnelling for the Metropolitan District Railway was by "cut and cover", as shown here in Leinster Gardens, Bayswater. The demolished houses were replaced with false facades to match the rest of the terrace, rather than impose too much weight over the shallow tunnel. Some 140,000,000 bricks were needed for the project, and in the middle of 1866 it was employing 2,000 men, 200 horses, and 58 steam engines. The line was finished in just four years and extended to Mansion House station in 1871.

The earliest means of public transport on the roads were sedan chairs and coaches. They were regulated from 1696 to restrict the trade to licensed chairmen and coachmen and protect the public from overcharging and abuse. They were called "Hackney" chairs and coaches, said to be named for the frequent journeys of City men to that popular suburban village. By 1813, on the eve of London's great expansion, there were 1,100 hackney coaches and still 400 sedan chairs for hire, though chairs would soon be phased out. Even the coaches were largely replaced by the dashing hansom cab, described by Benjamin Disraeli in 1870 as "the gondola of London".

The London bus, the first vehicle to move Londoners *en masse*, first took to the streets on July 4, 1829. The early omnibuses were drawn by two or three horses and carried up to 22 passengers. At sixpence a trip they were not for the poorest. Indeed, it was only later in the nineteenth century that the bus would become a working-class mode of transport.

ABOVE A model of the port of Roman London around AD 100. A new quay is being built into the river, replacing an earlier timber-faced one. Cargoes are being unloaded and stored in the warehouses along the waterfront.

The mechanical revolution of the twentieth century finally displaced the horse as the dominant means of carriage and haulage in London. The last horse bus ended service on the day the First World War broke out, August 4, 1914. Horse-drawn trams running on rails set into the roadway had given way to electrified services around a decade before. With the increase in motorized vehicles and the growth of London, the suburban bus network spread like a spider's web over the metropolis. The use of public transport became truly popular. In 1937–38, some 2.2 billion journeys were made in Greater London by bus and coach alone, twice the 1922 figure. The red Routemaster bus (introduced in 1956) would become – like the black taxicab – a London icon recognized throughout the world.

By that time, of course, road had long had to compete with rail in the options open to Londoners for getting around their city. The first London railway station opened at the south side of London Bridge in December 1836. With the growth of London, the importance of a suburban network to bring workers to jobs at the centre would become increasingly apparent. By 1854, some 54,000 City workers and visitors travelled by rail each day, though that number was dwarfed by the 400,000 who still walked in.

Soon after that, London's transit system was supplemented once more, for London became home to the world's first underground railway. It would grow to be the largest and busiest too, with "the tube" becoming the most characteristic way of getting around London. The first section opened in January 1863. It was still at that time steam railway, but it was electrification that would revolutionize the tube in the early years of the twentieth century, a process led by a buccaneering American entrepreneur, Charles Tyson Yerkes. Even after London stopped growing, the network continued to reach out in all directions. By the beginning of the twenty-first century, it had twelve lines, 268 stations, and carried 1,014 million passengers a year.

For those who wanted to get away from London, air travel proved an increasingly popular mode of transport. London's main airport, Heathrow, opened in 1946. Sixty years on it was the world's busiest, handling over 67 million passengers a year. Many of them would be strangers visiting London as tourists. But many would come to stay.

See also facsimile item 3 in envelope 1, opposite page 20.

RIGHT A traffic jam in Oxford Street. In 2003, the London Congestion Charge first made drivers pay to enter central London, but it seems traffic is a problem which London will never satisfactorily solve.

Londoners from Everywhere

For its first 1,000 years, London was a city of invaders. It owed its very existence to foreign conquerors. When the Romans left, they would be replaced by new invaders, the Anglo-Saxons (or English) from across the North Sea. In turn, the Danes and Vikings fought the English for sovereignty from the mid-ninth century on. In the tenth century, the Danes' quarter was on the Westminster side of the old City. Finally, after the conquest of 1066, the Normans turned London and Westminster into a European metropolis, including a sizeable Jewish minority in the heart of the City.

For its second millennium, London was a city of settlers. Its port brought sailors from most of the known world. Its bustling industries seduced skilled makers of luxury goods – jewellers, sword-makers, gilders – from mainland Europe. Foreign mercenaries helped fill the London garrisons. Men and women from Britain and Ireland sought work and prosperity in the giant city. Most important of all, the world's merchants, from Europe and the shores of the Mediterranean as far as the Bosphorus, settled in this great mart of commerce. Prominent among them were the Hanseatic merchants of Germany, the Genoese, the French and the Lombards (famous as moneylenders).

Many of the second generation of these settlers helped swell the ranks of the "cockneys", as the London born and bred seem to have been called since at least the time of the Stuarts. Their distinctive dialect and way with words found its way into stage plays from that time too. The cockneys were known for their quick wit, their sharp-eyed awareness of everything going on around them, their restless energy, materialism and vulgar flashy taste. Most typical of all cockney employments was the costermonger – the street seller and market trader. From the 1880s a new cockney "tradition" was implanted when costermongers took to sewing pearl buttons on their jackets and caps. The Pearlies became a tourist symbol of the Londoner for the next 100 years or so, a Pearly King and Queen being chosen from their number to reign as a cockney royal family.

Side-by-side with the cockney, wave after wave of migrants flowed into London from the provinces of Britain, Ireland and further afield. From 1685, the Huguenots, persecuted Protestant refugees from Catholic France, settled, especially in Soho and Spitalfields. Former slaves from the West Indies and the American colonies arrived in their hundreds, especially when the American Revolutionary War ended in 1783. A small armada of former slaves sailed from London soon afterwards to establish a new African country, Sierra Leone, with generally disastrous results for the first settlers. In the nineteenth century, European migrations planted distinctive foreign quarters in London: the French in Soho; the Germans in Whitechapel and Fitzrovia; the Italians in Holborn and Clerkenwell. From even further away, the Chinese settled in Limehouse. Most notable of all, perhaps as many as 100,000 East European Jews settled in the inner East End of London, mainly in the period 1881 to 1905.

All these were sideshows compared to the enormous change in the complexion of the Londoner that took place after the Second World

ABOVE A Jewish seller of old clothes, wearing several hats and a patched greatcoat, bargains with a butcher in an 1807 print by Robert Dighton. He seems to be offering a bonnet in exchange for some meat.

RIGHT The opium den made famous by Charles Dickens in *The Mystery of Edwin Drood*, captured by Gustave Doré around 1870. The opium users are Chinese and "Lascars", seamen from Malaysia and the Indian subcontinent.

ABOVE A disabled black man sells potted plants from a horse-drawn cart in a print of around 1810. By the late eighteenth century, increasing numbers of impoverished black people could be seen on London's streets, many of them freed slaves who had fought for the British against the American colonists.

RIGHT Pearly King and Queen outfits, worn between 1920 and 1961 by Frederick and Sarah Cole of Islington. The dress is in black velvet and both costumes are elaborately decorated in mother-of-pearl buttons.

BELOW RIGHT A young Italian street musician playing the harp, one of a talented musical family who had settled in Deptford (1877). There were numerous Italian street musicians specializing in popular song and operatic melodies at this time.

War. From 1948, migrants from former or existing British colonies claimed their right to the citizenship that the Empire had seemed to promise them. The arrival in London that year of 430 Jamaican men on the SS Empire Windrush proved a symbolic moment, duly captured on newsreel for posterity. First from the West Indies, then from Africa and the Indian subcontinent, hundreds of thousands of migrants came to make new lives in Britain. A high proportion settled in London, its vast size somehow helping ease the difficulties of settlement. London had also long been accustomed to accepting strangers within its boundaries, although acceptance would not always be easy for newcomers or cockneys alike. A few days of rioting against black newcomers in Notting Hill in the summer of 1958 could have been worse than in fact was the case. But assaults against individuals because of racial or cultural difference would prove harder to eliminate from the daily reality of London life.

By the twenty-first century, London was one of the great multicultural cities of the world – perhaps, indeed, the most mixed and most successful of all. By then, only around 60 per cent of Londoners were British-born. The rest would come from every nation and every race under the sun. And somewhere among the 7.5 million Londoners would be those who were making their way, like every generation before them, into London's Hall of Fame.

ABOVE Soho was traditionally the most "foreign" district of London from its first growth in the late seventeenth century. Italians are still a strong element in this extraordinarily cosmopolitan district, which also houses a world-famous Chinese community.

CARNIVAL CITY

The West Indian migration to London began in force a few years after the end of the Second World War, with the arrival of some 500 – mainly Jamaican – migrants on the SS Empire Windrush on June 22, 1948. By the early 1960s there were probably 100,000 West Indians in London, bringing with them a uniquely vibrant culture in which music played a special part. The carnival tradition from Trinidad quickly transplanted to London soil. Since 1965 the Notting Hill Carnival, held on every August Bank Holiday, has become one of the great events of the London calendar. It epitomizes the highly successful multicultural city that London has become in such an astonishingly short space of time.

London's Hall of Fame

The list of famous people who have been Londoners for all or some of their lives is endless and it continues to grow. Here are just a few who have left an enduring mark on their city. Richard (Dick) Whittington is a legend – so much so that many think he never existed at all. He was born around 1350 in Gloucestershire and apprenticed to a London mercer, or merchant in silks and luxury goods. He became one of the richest men of his age. Whittington's wealth and wisdom made him Mayor in 1397, 1406 and 1419. A charitable man, he left his fortune to the city and the citizens he loved. The legend of Dick Whittington – of the cat that made his fortune by killing all the rats in his master's ship, and the chime of Bow Bells that told him to "Turn again Whittington, Lord Mayor of London" – were common fare by the 1600s, two hundred years after his death (in 1423).

William Shakespeare (1564–1616) was born into a prosperous family in Stratford-upon-Avon. He became an actor there, and a playwright. Facts are sparse but he was certainly in London by 1592 and it was there that he established his reputation as perhaps the greatest Englishman of all time. By 1599 he was living near the Globe Theatre on Bankside, and until the end of his life London provided the stage on which he worked and lived. The common people of London populate his dramas, whether placed in medieval Scotland or Renaissance Venice. And the monument to Shakespeare's London, the new Globe Theatre, completed in 1997, has become an internationally famous memorial to his art.

Samuel Pepys (1633–1703), the greatest of English diarists, was the only one of our gallery born in London, at Salisbury Court, Fleet Street, in 1633. His father was a master tailor. Educated at St Paul's School and then a self-supporting student at Cambridge, Pepys became a public official in the Navy Office. But it is his extraordinary diary for which he is immortal. For Pepys was an active witness to some of the greatest dramas of London's long history; he lived through the plague year of 1665 and, in 1666, the Great Fire which obliterated much of the City of London. His eye-witness accounts are uniquely vivid because so personally felt. He survived into the new century, dying in 1703.

Elizabeth Fry (1780–1845), one of the greatest philanthropists of her age, was born in Norwich in 1780 into a Quaker family. On her marriage in 1800, she moved to London, at first to the City and later to suburban East Ham. It was when she became aware of the desperate conditions of the women prisoners in Newgate that her philanthropy found its real purpose. From 1816, braving disease and resistance from every quarter, she established a school for the children imprisoned with their mothers, then educational classes, proper clothing and paid work for the women. Until her death in 1845, she inspired others to work with women prisoners and to establish enduring institutions for their welfare.

Charles Dickens (1812–70), the writer with whose name London will always be twinned, was born in Portsmouth in 1812 and first moved to London with his family at the age of ten. His father was notoriously improvident and his debts landed him in the Marshalsea Prison in Southwark. The young Dickens lodged nearby and the experiences of that time are wryly recalled in *David Copperfield* and *Little Dorrit*. His *Bleak House* (1852–53) opens with the single word "London", and the city and its people was the true obsession of his transcendent genius. Dickens died too young,

worn out with endless hard work, in 1870. Another London novel – *The Mystery of Edwin Drood* – lay unfinished on his desk.

Sir Winston Churchill (1874–1965), the greatest Englishman of the twentieth century, was born at Blenheim Palace in 1874 and educated at Harrow School in north-west London. Careers as a soldier and a journalist, and as MP for a northern constituency, were combined with permanent residence in London. Churchill was a consummate metropolitan with an eye for the main chance: he was, indeed, an archetypal cockney in everything but birth. Perhaps his American speculator grandfather had contributed to his sharp wit and steely backbone. It was this last characteristic that proved of monumental worth. It was Churchill, not alone but above all, who helped Londoners pull through the Blitz of 1940–41. For this (and much else) he would be gratefully remembered until the end of his long life in 1965.

ABOVE Dick Whittington the legend, as perpetrated by the publisher Raphael Tuck around 1895. Whittington became a model of individual enterprise and the capacity to rise within society, in his case from poor apprentice to Lord Mayor of London.

OPPOSITE FAR LEFT The reconstructed Globe Theatre on the South Bank of the Thames, the dream of the American actor-director Sam Wanamaker, opened in 1997. It successfully recreated one of the great Southwark theatres of early seventeenth-century London.

OPPOSITE LEFT Shakespeare's arrival in London in 1592 was ill timed, the theatres being largely closed because of a plague from 1592–94. This portrait once hung in the actors' room at Sadler's Wells.

BELOW Sir Winston Churchill leaves London for the last time on January 30, 1965. His coffin was taken from Waterloo Station to the family seat of the Churchills at Blenheim Palace, Oxfordshire.

RIGHT Elizabeth Fry's entry pass into Newgate Prison. Fry's pass gave her entrance to the Female Side, filled with thieves and prostitutes. Across Fry's pass lies the key to the execution door at Newgate.

BELOW RIGHT Writing tools from the age of Samuel Pepys, the greatest diarist in English literature and a Londoner born and bred. The copy of Pepys's *State of the Royal Navy* (1690) is said to have belonged to William IV.

DICKENS THE LONDONER

Charles Dickens was London's greatest-ever fictional chronicler. His art was founded on a childhood and youth made dramatic by an improvident father who landed the family in the Marshalsea Prison in Southwark for debt in 1824, when Charles was twelve years old. Early employment in a blacking factory near the Thames deeply scarred his childhood and he had no sustained education. His *Sketches by Boz*, begun in the *Monthly Magazine* from December 1833, made his reputation at the age of twenty-one. *The Pickwick Papers* made him immortal three years later – a Pickwickians commemorative handkerchief from around 1839 is pictured here.

Crown and Capital

An unbroken connection between royalty and London now goes back nearly 1,000 years. There were likely to have been royal palaces in the City even before that, but it is the settlement of Edward the Confessor at Westminster in 1042 from which the lineage can certainly be dated. He built a palace there close to his great Abbey church of St Peter. The first coronation at Westminster Abbey was that of Harold on January 6, 1066; the second was that of William the Conqueror on Christmas Day of that same year. Most of the kings and queens of England have been crowned there ever since, in the Abbey magnificently rebuilt by Henry III from 1245.

The Palace of Westminster, established by the Confessor, was added to and rebuilt over succeeding centuries. Like all London, these great buildings were permanently vulnerable to fire, and in 1512 the palace was badly damaged in a blaze which dispersed the royal household to several buildings around London. In 1529, Henry VIII secured a new home for the court at York House (or Place), the splendid former residence of the Archbishops of York, and renamed it the Palace of Whitehall. It sprawled along the riverfront from Scotland Yard to St James's Park and contained over 1,000 apartments with cockpit, indoor tennis court, chapel, a massive gallery and huge rooms for entertaining. The Tudor buildings fell into disrepair and Whitehall was partly rebuilt by James I, to the designs of Inigo Jones, from 1613. Jones's magnificent Banqueting Hall still survives, but his grandiose and far-sighted projection for an entirely new palace was never built.

Of all the London palaces, Whitehall saw the most drama. Elizabeth was imprisoned there in 1544 for her part in a conspiracy against the Catholic tendencies of her older half-sister Queen Mary. At the close of her reign, Elizabeth presided over enormous entertainments there with her "wrinkled face, a red periwig, little eyes, a hooked nose, shining lips, and black teeth". Half a century later, on January 30, 1649, Charles I would be led to Whitehall to be beheaded in front of an enormous crowd. After the deed was done, the second executioner held up the head to the throng: "Behold the head of a traitor!"

ABOVE An 1859 portrait of Queen Victoria (aged 40) by Franz Xaver Winterhalter, a fashionable court artist. Victoria had been queen since 1837 when she was just 17, and had become a popular monarch by the time this portrait was painted.

LEFT A tin-glazed earthenware plate commemorating the accession of William III and Mary in 1689. The new reign re-established Protestantism as the national religion and irrevocably shifted the balance of power from Crown to parliament with the Bill of Rights of 1689.

ABOVE The Regalia of Charles II on the Restoration of the Monarchy in 1660, including the Crown of State and the Royal Sceptre.

LEFT Oliver Cromwell triumphing over the corpse of Charles I, January 1649. Many legends attached to Cromwell's role in the regicide and this is a Victorian imagining of a scene which probably never happened.

BELOW The funeral cortège of Diana, Princess of Wales, passing Buckingham Palace on September 6, 1997. Hundreds of thousands of people lined the processional route.

Whitehall Palace was destroyed in a disastrous fire in January 1698 and the court moved to St James's Palace, an irregular brick building dating from Henry VIII's time. It would be the main royal palace until George IV rebuilt Buckingham Palace (formerly Buckingham House) and William IV moved the court there in the 1830s. Since 1837, Buckingham Palace has remained the royal residence of the sovereign when in London.

If royal palaces have made up some of London's most historic and prestigious buildings, royal events have punctuated the city's daily life and provided its greatest pageants. The coronation and wedding of George III on September 22, 1761 drew vast crowds to Westminster, not just from London, but the nation at large. The procession from Westminster Hall to the Abbey took place along a specially built raised way, covered with blue cloth. Thousands took part in a spectacle of unparalleled magnificence. The royal party were preceded by "the King's herb woman" and six maids strewing sweet herbs. A marching band, the sheriffs, aldermen and Lord Mayor of London, the judges and great officers of state, hundreds of choristers, ceremonial officers of the court, peers of the realm in order of precedence, the nation's crown jewels carried on velvet cushions, the royal couple under separate canopies of cloth of gold each held aloft by 16 barons – nothing like this had been seen in living memory or would occur again for generations to come. Indeed, the Imperial London of Queen Victoria, who reigned from 1837 to 1901, was muted by comparison, especially after the death of her beloved Prince Albert in 1861.

Royal occasions would continue to provide the greatest pageants in the life of modern London. The coronation of Elizabeth II in 1953 was the first such ceremony to be televised. It was watched all over the world. The Queen's golden coach was breathtaking, even though this was the only coronation in history to suffer from a shortage of coachmen. London's traditional pageantry goes on delighting both Londoners and the world's tourists whenever a visiting head of state is escorted to Buckingham Palace. Perhaps London does these things better than anywhere else, exactly because the traditions have such a long and distinguished history.

See also facsimile items 4 and 5 in envelope 2, opposite page 48.

BELOW Charles II's jubilant procession through the City of London on April 22, 1661, the day before his Coronation. The new king's pageant is seen wending its way through specially erected triumphal arches, though the City streets and populace are nowhere to be seen.

City and Parliament

The government of Roman London was sophisticated and complex but its details remain sketchy. A postal service, tax-gatherers, law and customs officers, and the governor and financial minister of Britannia all had special buildings to themselves. Official public residences lay close to the river, but London government was directed from the basilica, or city hall, north of the bridge.

In Saxon times, wards were established in London and these became the basis of medieval City government by the twelfth century. William the Conqueror confirmed the City's rights to make its own laws. The wardmotes or local citizen gatherings elected common councilmen and a single alderman to represent them in the City's "courts" or councils. A Mayor was elected from among the aldermen each year and acted as the King's deputy and chief magistrate. The first whose name has come down to us is Henry Fitz Ailwin, a cloth merchant, who served from 1189. The earliest description of a Mayor's Pageant or Show, the ceremonial visit paid by the new Mayor to the monarch at Westminster, dates from 1236. Each pageant was a prodigious display of the wealth of the aldermen – the richest merchants in England.

London city government predated the English Parliament, which emerged in the thirteenth century. From January 1265, parliaments began to assume their present form, meeting frequently at the Great Hall in the Palace of Westminster. This would be their permanent home from 1483. The Houses of Parliament would continue to be known as the Palace of Westminster.

That Palace was nearly destroyed, together with James I and all the peers and commoners, in an act of terrorism planned to take place on November 5, 1605. A party of disaffected Catholics, among them Guido (Guy) Fawkes, hired a cellar beneath the parliament building and secreted 20 barrels of gunpowder, coals and firewood there. By good fortune, or through betrayal, the "Gunpowder Plot" was discovered. After terrible tortures, eight of the plotters were hanged, drawn and quartered outside St Paul's Cathedral and in Palace Yard, Westminster, in January 1606.

A generation later, Parliament and City would find themselves in alliance against an arrogant, dictatorial and importunate monarch, Charles I. A frustrated attempt to get the City to raise money provoked Charles to imprison four aldermen in the Tower in May 1640. Two years later and he would try to arrest the leading Parliamentarians, summoned to provide him with the funds he needed. The crisis between King and Parliament saw Charles make the fatal mistake of leaving London for the country in January 1642. The citizens began to arm themselves in preparation for an attack by Royalist armies – the original "roundheads" were City apprentices with their close-cropped hair. The Civil War broke out that August. It would be seven years before Charles saw London again – just days before his trial and execution in 1649.

Parliament and the City would not always see eye to eye. A hundred years on and to the citizens of London it seemed that Parliament had become as domineering and unreasonable as any monarch. When Parliament prosecuted some printers for reporting Parliamentary speeches, proceedings were obstructed by

ABOVE The Lord Mayor's Dinner at Guildhall in 1829. These dinners were given each year by the incoming Lord Mayor for the Aldermen, Common Council and prominent guests, and were famous for their unrestrained gluttony

ABOVE A river view of the Houses of Parliament or Palace of Westminster. A stunning architectural triumph, the Houses of Parliament have become among the most recognizable buildings in the world.

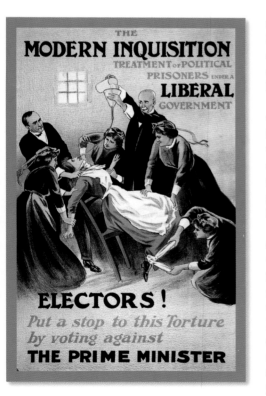

ABOVE A Women's Social and Political Union Poster, c.1910, protesting against the force-feeding of suffragette prisoners on hunger strike.

the City magistrates who refused to allow the arrest warrants to be enforced. An outraged Parliament committed the Lord Mayor and an alderman to the Tower in the spring of 1771. Riots and rumours of riots plagued much of the relations between City and Parliament around this time.

On the night of October 16, 1834, both Houses of Parliament were completely destroyed by an accidental fire. Rebuilding began in 1840 and took more than 20 years to complete. The designer was Charles Barry, the greatest London architect of the age, with decoration in the Gothic style by Augustus Pugin. The great clock tower, with its giant hour bell named Big Ben after a prominent government minister Sir Benjamin Hall, was fully operational by 1860.

The Houses of Parliament have witnessed many historic scenes since, and have been the cause of drama beyond their walls. Few were more bitter than the struggles over women's right to vote. From 1908 to 1914 in particular, suffragettes chained themselves to Parliament's railings, rioted in Downing Street, stoned the Guildhall during the Lord Mayor's banquet, mobbed the Prime Minister, smashed West End shop windows, exploded bombs, set fires and even tried to blow up St Paul's Cathedral. Women over the age of 30 would be given the vote in 1918 and full adult suffrage granted in 1928. But the suffragettes remind us that politics and riot have frequently gone hand in hand.
See also facsimile item 6 in envelope 2, opposite page 48.

See also facsimile item 6 in envelope 2, opposite page 48.

London pageantry has not only been the prerogative of the Crown: the City too has a long tradition of gorgeous processions for the delight of the citizens. The earliest show or pageant put on by the City Companies was recorded in 1298, and the annual Lord Mayor's Show emerged from these festivities and in the visit by the new Mayor to the king at Westminster after the annual election in October (later November). In 1757, a magnificent new coach was designed for the Lord Mayor, beautifully carved and gilded. The allegorical painted panels depicting the City's commercial activities have been attributed to Giovanni Battista Cipriani, one of many European artists at work in London in the eighteenth century.

Konig Carolus.

BANCKET HAVS.

Der Gerechten Seelen sein in Gottes hand.

Gen: Fairfax.

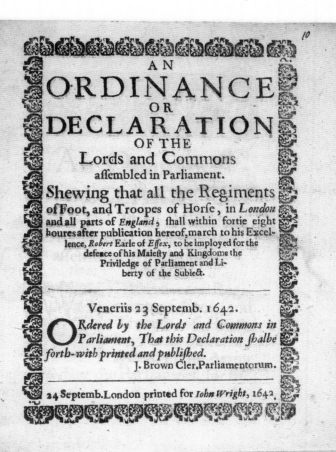

AN
ORDINANCE
OR
DECLARATION
OF THE
Lords and Commons
assembled in Parliament.
Shewing that all the Regiments
of Foot, and Troopes of Horse, in *London*
and all parts of *England*; shall within fortie eight
houres after publication hereof, march to his Excellence, *Robert* Earle of *Essex*, to be imployed for the
defence of his Maiesty and Kingdome the
Priviledge of Parliament and Li-
berty of the Subiect.

Veneriis 23 Septemb. 1642.
ORdered by the Lords and Commons in
Parliament, That this Declaration shalbe
forth-with printed and published.
J. Brown Cler. Parliamentorum.

24 Septemb. London printed for *Iohn Wright*, 1642.

ABOVE The Parliamentary Ordinance of September 23, 1642 requiring all troops in London and elsewhere to assemble under the leadership of Robert, Earl of Essex, the Parliamentary commander. Londoners, fearful that Charles might seek to re-enter their city, mobilized in citizen armies or Trained Bands.

LEFT A contemporary German print showing the execution of Charles I. His beheading took place on a stage erected before the Banqueting House in Whitehall.

Politics and Riot

In the year 60, Boudicca, Queen of the Iceni, led a revolt against Roman rule in eastern Britain. The Britons overran what is now Essex in such numbers that the Romans abandoned London to its fate. Those who remained were massacred, by all accounts in brutal and pitiless circumstances. London was then put to the torch. The traces of this first great fire can still be seen, four metres (13 feet) or more below London's pavements, in a layer of baked red clay from its wattle and daub walls, some half a metre (20 inches) thick.

This event, so early in the city's life, would never be repeated. There were, though, terrible upheavals. The Peasants' Revolt of 1381 saw thousands of Kentish and Essex rebels descend on London to air their grievances to the king. Led by Wat Tyler and given spiritual support by a renegade priest, John Ball, their mood was uncompromising. They sacked Lambeth Palace, residence of the Archbishop of Canterbury, looted the Savoy Palace and even stormed the Tower of London. They beheaded any noble or official they could find, the Archbishop among them. At Smithfield, the rebels met Richard II for negotiations, but in a fracas Tyler was severely wounded by the Mayor, William Walworth. The king claimed sovereignty over the leaderless rebels and turned them away from London.

In 1450, the men of Kent were on the march again. This time their leader was Jack Cade, an Irish adventurer who amassed 20,000 men to redress popular grievances against royal mismanagement. He camped at Blackheath and his strength of numbers was such that the City gates had to be opened to him. The rebels stayed in and around London for some days, while Henry VI fled with his court to Kenilworth in the Midlands. Eventually a majority of citizens tired of their unwanted visitors and denied them entry with force of arms. Great numbers were killed on both sides. Cade was forced to replenish his army from the Southwark gaols, but when they were offered a royal indemnity, Cade's forces left him to his fate. Found hiding in a Sussex garden, he was later put to the sword.

OPPOSITE The hustings for a Parliamentary election at Westminster in 1818, from a painting by George Scharf. He captures well the sheer celebratory fun of the occasion as voters poll in public before their neighbours.

ABOVE The Gordon Riots, Broad Street, City, on the evening of Wednesday June 7, 1780. These riots were the most violent disturbance in London for centuries, when the city really did appear on the verge of civil war.

RIGHT A baselard or short sword from the time of the Peasants' Revolt. The Mayor William Walworth drew a baselard and inflicted a serious wound on Wat Tyler at Smithfield in the final moments of the Revolt.

FAR RIGHT A left-wing pamphlet issued in the wake of the Brixton Riots of April 10–12, 1981. Some 261 police officers were injured and 145 buildings were damaged in the riots, mainly by fire.

POLICE OUT OF BRIXTON!

30p

South London Workers Against Racism

In later centuries, trouble would come from the Londoners themselves. Foreigners were often a source of discontent, and "foreigners" meant anyone who was not a citizen of London. In 1517, the large numbers of non-Londoners who set up trade just beyond the City boundaries were such an economic threat that apprentices and citizens took to desperate measures. On "Evil May-Day", once more encouraged by a ferocious clergyman, Dr Bell, they plundered and burned the outsiders' homes, warehouses and shops. A dozen or so rioters were hanged on moveable gibbets to deter any repetition of the outrage.

A far more serious affair took place a quarter of a millennium later. In June 1780, a demonstration led by Lord George Gordon presented a petition to Parliament to restore restrictions on Catholics, which had recently been repealed. It turned to furious rioting, unique in modern times. For a full week, rioters proclaiming "No Popery" seemed to have London at their mercy. The homes and businesses of prominent Catholics and Papist chapels were destroyed. Newgate and other prisons were emptied of their inmates and burned. The homes of magistrates and judges who had aggrieved the people were sacked and looted. Belatedly, in the face of a rumoured attack on the Bank of England, troops were ordered to shoot to kill. Unknown numbers, at least 200, were killed in the streets and 21 were hanged after the event.

The Gordon Riots saw London at war with itself. In the more than two centuries since, nothing like it has been seen again. Yet riot remained a feature of London's political life until the end of the nineteenth century. Riots in favour of parliamentary reform broke out occasionally from 1819 to 1866. Fierce riots of unemployed workers and their socialist sympathizers in February 1886 caused "an absolute panic" for two or three days, made worse by a thick "pea-soup" fog. The twentieth century proved quieter but not quiescent. The Battle of Cable Street on October 4, 1936 saw ugly scenes when police tried to force a way through crowds determined to prevent Fascists marching through the Jewish East End. And the worst disorder of the last half-century, at Brixton in April 1981, had a virulent anti-police component when youths – many but not all of them black – fought the Metropolitan Police, causing considerable damage to property.

It looked for a time as though London was at war with itself once more. By then, though, London had already witnessed more than enough of the real thing.

NOTICE.

MEETINGS IN TRAFALGAR SQUARE.

In consequence of the disorderly scenes which have recently occurred in Trafalgar Square, and of the danger to the peace of the Metropolis from meetings held there, and with a view to prevent such disorderly proceedings, and to preserve the peace :—

I, CHARLES WARREN, the Commissioner of Police of the Metropolis, do hereby give Notice, with the sanction of the Secretary of State, and the concurrence of the Commissioners of Her Majesty's Works and Public Buildings, that, until further intimation, no Public Meetings will be allowed to assemble in Trafalgar Square, nor will speeches be allowed to be delivered therein; and all well-disposed persons are hereby cautioned and requested to abstain from joining or attending any such Meeting or Assemblage; and Notice is further given that all necessary measures will be adopted to prevent any such Meeting or Assemblage, or the delivery of any speech, and effectually to preserve the Public peace, and to suppress any attempt at the disturbance thereof.

This Notice is not intended to interfere with the use by the Public of Trafalgar Square for all ordinary purposes, or to affect the Regulations issued by me with respect to Lord Mayor's Day.

Metropolitan Police Office,
4, Whitehall Place,
8th November, 1887.

CHARLES WARREN,
The Commissioner of Police of the Metropolis.

Printed by McCorquodale & Company Limited, "The Armoury," Southwark. 17244

London at War

Londoners have known wars throughout their history. They have generally acquitted themselves well, but not always: during the Wars of the Roses, 1455–85, Londoners' loyalties ebbed and flowed according to whoever seemed to be coming out on top. At one time they swore allegiance – and opened their purses – to the house of York and at another to Lancaster, the two families contending for the throne of England. And then back again; they were serial turncoats. Londoners helped the usurper Richard III (a Yorkist) take power in 1483 – it was he who allegedly murdered the princes in the Tower. And in 1485, with equal enthusiasm, they welcomed the "rebel" Henry VII, whose forces had defeated and slain Richard in battle.

The Londoners' collective eye to the main chance would not be entirely absent in the next great tumult, the Civil War of 1642 to 1651. In its public utterances, the City was on Parliament's side. A great ring of forts and earthworks was thrown round London by voluntary labour. There would be "mounds" in London for some 200 years to come where these forts had been. The London "Trained Bands", or citizen militia, were called out to secure the capital against the king's army. But as the splits within the Parliamentary ranks grew wider, with a radical army wanting to proclaim a republic, many citizens, in contrast, favoured an accommodation with the king. The army, through a show of strength, proved in the end most persuasive of all. The insecurity of the times encouraged a custom that would have an enduring effect on City life: the banking habit, with merchants lodging their cash in the safe hands of the goldsmiths, became prevalent in the 1640s.

But it was in the century of total war that London would come into its own. The First World War of 1914–18 had a giant impact on London. In general, and perhaps surprisingly, it was progressive. The war gave a mighty push forward to the urban growth and economic capacity of London. Both the interwar suburbs and the strength of London manufacturing were largely the product of the better living standards and widened horizons for women that the war created. Many of these effects were long lasting. There was a setback, though, and it came within a generation.

RIGHT The Bank Underground Station tragedy, January 10, 1941. That night, the station received a direct hit during a heavy air raid. Some 111 people were killed. Royal Engineers cleared the crater and bridged it in just three weeks.

On September 3, 1939, Britain declared war on Germany. That same month, the greatest and most complex plan ever devised for the movement of people in Britain went into operation. Some 660,000 women and children were moved out of London to protect them from the bombing that was thought to be imminent. In fact, the bombs did not fall for almost a year. The bombing began almost by accident: on August 24, 1940, a night-time German raid on London occurred through error, bad luck or mischief, provoking retaliation on Berlin by the RAF. On September 7, 1940, "Black Saturday", all hell broke loose. The London Blitz had begun. Almost every night until May 13, 1941, London was bombed, sometimes ferociously. The worst City fire since 1666 took place just a couple of nights before the end of this first stage. There would be other phases almost to the end of the war in Europe, including attacks by "flying bombs" (or V1s) and by terrifying rockets, the V2s. In all, nearly 30,000 Londoners were killed and over 50,000 seriously injured. The damage to property was enormous. Some 116,000 houses were destroyed, 288,000 seriously damaged; 2,000,000 required repair. The effects on some aspects of London's economic life – the docks and manufacturing in central London – would be permanent. Even so, the war proved the Cockney's finest hour, for Londoners epitomized the resilience and cheerful heroism of the British at war.

Finally, London's war on terrorism. In the late nineteenth century, Londoners had to cope with Irish terrorism – including bombs on the Underground in 1883 – and foreign anarchists. A Frenchman had tried to blow up Greenwich Observatory in 1894 but succeeded only in blowing up himself. The Irish bombed on into the twentieth century. From 1973 to 1996, they did so with shocking destruction of life and property. There were also isolated outrages by Middle-Eastern terrorists between 1977 and 1984.

When the 9/11 attacks on New York's World Trade Center stunned the globe in 2001, many Londoners reckoned that it would only be a matter of time before their own city would be targeted. They were right. On July 7, 2005 ("7/7"), 52 Londoners were killed by co-ordinated bomb-blasts on the Underground system and on a London bus. The future required vigilance if some sort of repetition were to be avoided.

ABOVE The first air raid on London was made by a single Zeppelin airship on May 31, 1915 – seven people were killed and 32 injured. This recruitment poster of around 1916 encouraged men to enlist as the best way of stopping the raids.

OPPOSITE The Fenian Brotherhood of Irish Republicans bombed London between 1883 and 1885. In October 1883, a bomb was dropped from a moving Underground train, injuring 72 passengers. The blast was felt on Praed Street Station, Paddington.

ABOVE The scene at South Quay, near Canary Wharf in London's Docklands, after the detonation of a massive bomb by the IRA on February 10, 1996. Two men died and around 40 were injured.

LEFT It was generally expected on the outbreak of war in 1939 that gas would be used against civilians. The importance of telephony in wartime led to the creation of special gas masks for telephonists. Fortunately, they were never needed.

London's River

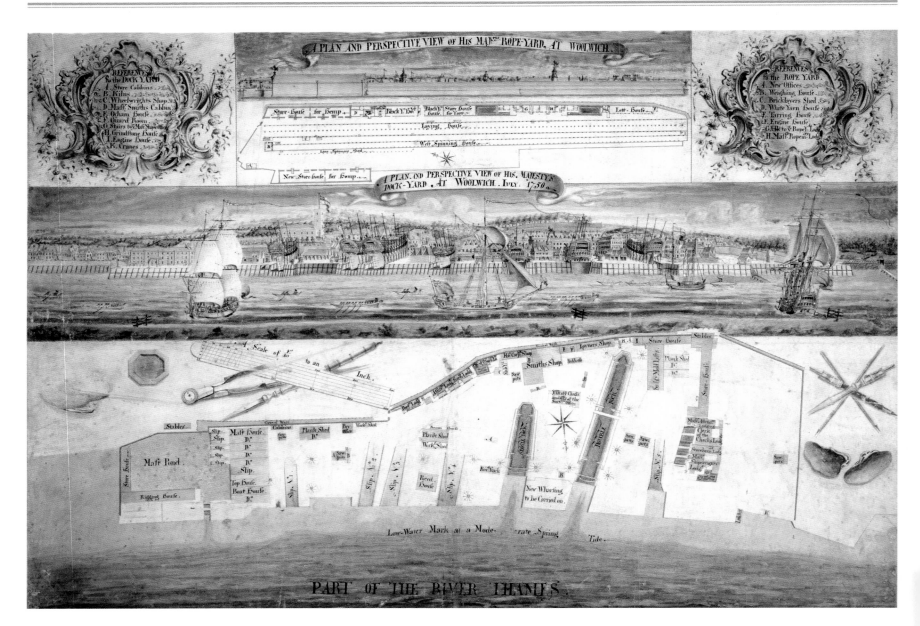

Londinium, the capital of Rome's northernmost province, had necessarily to be a port, in touch with the luxuries of Rome and in swift reach of its armies and supplies. From the beginning, the Thames was its lifeblood, bringing pottery and wine from Italy and Gaul, oil from Spain and exotic marble from Greece and Egypt.

For the first 1,000 years, the port of London was a harbour in an extensive marshy estuary, the river sluggish and broad. Towards the end of this period, the main quayside was at Queenhithe, up from London Bridge, and another was downriver at Billingsgate. Reclamation of the City's north bank at Thames Street was one of London's great developments from the twelfth to the fifteenth centuries. Along it were built quays and wharves and warehouses. At this time, if not before, London became one of the greatest ports in the western world, the leading shipper of woollen cloth to the whole of Europe.

But the Thames proved temperamental. It was, by virtue of its overseas trade, a great boon, and by virtue of its opportunities for leisure and display, a great source of pride. But every few winters or so, its tides would swell through wind and rain, and Westminster, Southwark and parts of the City flooded, sometimes disastrously. The last tragic Thames flood was as late as January 1928: fourteen Londoners drowned in their beds. And before embankments were extensively in place from the mid-nineteenth century, the turgid river would freeze from shore to shore and along great lengths, stifling the river's trade within a single hour. There are records of these freezing winters back to the thirteenth century at least; and we know that on numerous occasions, including 1683–84, 1715–16, 1739–40, 1788–89 and lastly 1813–14 the depth of ice was such that "Frost Fairs" brought out showmen and stallholders, and oxen were roasted on great open fires on the river.

OPPOSITE A plan and perspective of the massive Royal Dockyards at Woolwich, drawn and painted in 1750. His Majesty's Dockyard was established by Henry VIII in 1512–13 to build his giant flagship, the modestly named *Great Harry*.

RIGHT The giant gates of the Millwall Dock nearing completion in 1868. The Millwall Dock Company was formed in 1864 to build this enormous L-shaped wet dock, mainly for importing grain from the Baltic.

BELOW Frost Fair on the Thames at Temple Stairs, January 1684. The river froze from December 3 until February 4, and the ice was 28 centimetres (11 inches) thick. It was said that 40 coaches plied daily on the Thames as though it were dry land.

ABOVE Elephants from Chipperfield's Circus being carefully disembarked at South West India Dock in the Isle of Dogs after a tour of South Africa in 1968.

LEFT The river was one of London's great workplaces. These two men on a Thames sailing barge were photographed by John Thomson around 1877 for a book on *Street Life in London*, which described the river as the "Silent Highway".

From the sixteenth century, the growth of world trade forced the port of London to adapt to changing circumstances. During the reign of Henry VIII in particular, ships grew larger. To accommodate them, the riverside trades edged closer to the sea. Land was reclaimed from the river and embanked as far as Wapping. Around the same time, able to take advantage of the new facilities, great companies of City merchants combined to invest in trade with Russia and the Levant. In the seventeenth century, they would extend their reach to the East Indies and Africa and in 1711 to the "South Seas" (Central and South America).

It was the needs of trade that eventually caused a revolution in the port. At the turn of the nineteenth century, the need to service and repair great ocean-going ships, while keeping their cargoes secure from river pirates, drove merchants to fortify the riverside with a series of huge privately-owned docks and warehouses. As the upper

ABOVE "Manhattan-on-Thames", London's docklands at the turn of the twenty-first century. Developed from 1981, an astonishing new financial service and residential area grew out of the ruins of London's upper port.

port became cluttered, the docks companies reached for blue water downriver. First, in 1802, came the giant West India Docks on the Isle of Dogs, then the London Docks back at Wapping, followed by the great expansion of the old docks at Rotherhithe on the river's southern shore, all by 1815. The process would continue, upriver at St Katharine Docks and then far out from Blackwall to West and East Ham and eventually to deep water at Tilbury, 42 kilometres (26 miles) from London Bridge, in 1886.

The docks became one of London's great employers in the nineteenth and early twentieth centuries. In the earlier period, they gave work of last resort to the most wretched and decrepit of London's poor. The daily scramble for a day's or half a day's paid employment was one of London's most gruesome sights. There were many hard-fought struggles between the dock labourer and the dock owners – the Great Dock Strike for the "Docker's Tanner"

(sixpence an hour) in 1889 most notable among them.

When labour began to get a fairer deal, the men clung to their rights in a grip that stifled flexibility and innovation. Never were those qualities more needed than after the Second World War. Roll-on roll-off lorry traffic, carrying large freight containers from port to customer, posed special problems for the upper port, where roads had been built to accommodate just horse-drawn vehicles. Practical difficulties and labour intransigence offered no hope. After nearly 2,000 years' constant use, the upper port would gradually close in the space of just 14 years, from 1967 to 1981.

Since then, London's Docklands have been transformed into a "mini-Manhattan", one of the greatest financial services districts in the world. Docklands are like no other part of London. But in the long history of London, perhaps this transformation was just one more way of making money.

Making Money

FROM the beginning, Roman London was home to a significant minority of rich citizens. Their luxurious lifestyle has come down to us through delicate mosaics, ornate tombstones and brilliant jewellery. At times a mint was needed in London to supply coins to the army, and an official treasury, stashed with British precious metals, remained until the last Roman left. This gold and silver thread through London's story, spun first by trade and at last by the manipulation of the world's money supply, has survived some 2,000 years. And its spinning-wheel has long been located at the very heart of the City of London.

For many centuries that wealth was created from wool. London's woollen exports made its merchants and ship owners the richest commoners in Europe. When kings wanted money for crusades and wars, it was to the merchants of London that they came. Though kings and queens faced turmoil, and the crown itself lay in deadly dispute, the merchants of London went on amassing their gold. They hardly paused for breath. Under the Tudors, world trade flourished as never before. The growing numbers of merchants, and their ever-increasing desire for rapid "intelligence" or worldwide information, required an entirely new institution: the Royal Exchange, opened by Queen Elizabeth I in 1571. It was not only the powerful who recognized the authority of the City of London. In the turbulent years of Civil War in the 1640s, the goldsmiths of London – bankers in waiting – provided the best safe-keeping for a family's plate, jewels and coin.

BELOW A well-attended sale of imported goods at East India House, the Leadenhall Street headquarters of the East India Company, in 1808. Established in 1600, the Company held the sole rights to trade with what later became British India.

One London institution in particular became synonymous with City wealth. The East India Company was established in 1600 to facilitate British trade with India and the East Indies, from where it imported silks, muslins, spices and gems. More important, in the eighteenth century the Company was given licence to govern India, as much on its own behalf as on Britain's; certainly not on behalf of the Indians. Almost the whole of the subcontinent was ruled, not from Delhi or Calcutta, not even from St James's Palace or the Houses of Parliament, but from the Company's headquarters in Leadenhall Street. Its merchants, governors and military officers became some of the richest men in England, known – even in their London suburban mansions – as "Nabobs".

But making money in London was not all plain sailing. Sometimes greed over-reached itself. Across the centuries there were numerous financial crises, many fuelled by rash speculation. Most madcap of all was the South Sea Bubble of 1720. Through reckless financial mismanagement laced with fraud, the South Sea Company offered investors huge returns on their money when the Company's only income came not from trade, but from the purchase of shares by those eager for the dividend. Share prices rose to astronomical heights. When the Bubble burst, they fell more dramatically still. Overnight, thousands were ruined and tens of thousands left wondering where their money had gone. Many investors, unable to stand the shock, committed suicide. When the dust settled the scale of shareholding madness was revealed in dozens of smaller "bubbles", schemes so fanciful it seemed incredible that anyone could invest in them.

Crises like this proved incapable of destabilizing London's moneymaking capacity for long. Fraud and fantasy went hand in hand with the generally rising fortunes of London and the nation. The unparalleled technological advances of the nineteenth century produced endless opportunities for making profit, the railways key among them. These would have their own share-buying frenzy in the "Railway Mania" of 1846. New industries like electrical engineering and telegraphy were matched in their moneymaking potential by revolutionary changes in traditional industries like printing and clothing manufacture for mass markets. Even more astonishing was the place London won in world banking. Not just lenders now to the kings of England, London's bankers funded the aspirations of the whole British Empire and of governments right round the world. Many foreign nations, in South America and elsewhere, even had their banknotes printed in London.

Two World Wars left London's financial services shaken but unbowed. From the 1950s, culminating in "Big Bang" in October 1986, London championed flexibility in financial products and espoused competition as the basis of regulation. By the end of the twentieth century, London had established itself, with Tokyo and New York, as one of three great global financial centres or "World Cities". But London's reputation rested on more than making money. It involved spending it too.

See also facsimile items 7 and 8 in envelope 2, opposite page 48.

LEFT An eighteenth-century view of the bustle and informality of the Royal Exchange or 'Change, as it was known, where the merchants and financiers of the world met to transact business – agree prices, nominate a ship's captain, arrange insurance, or do a deal.

new streets were designed with shopping in mind. Regent Street at that time was the most spectacular shopping street in the world. There and elsewhere, shops exploited to the full the technologies of display, literally putting their goods in the best light: wax candles, oil reflectors and glass lustres in the early years, plate glass and gas light from the early nineteenth century. It was the shopkeepers of London who popularized the use of both gas and electricity and encouraged their spread into the homes of their customers.

From the late-seventeenth century, the idea slowly caught on of bringing different shops together under one roof. There were shops in the Royal Exchange (see p.48), and other "Exchanges" followed, but none prospered for long. A more fruitful plan was modelled on the eastern bazaar. First and longest lasting was the Soho Bazaar in Soho Square, opened by John Trotte=r in 1816. It was aimed especially at women, not just the customers but the proprietors of the scores of shops there, and their shop assistants too. The Bazaar encouraged browsing in a comfortable and secure environment. Here lay the origins of the department store and the shopping centre. The principle has withstood the test of time remarkably well.

The first London department store, Whiteley's, opened in Westbourne Grove as early as 1863, but it was Oxford Street which would prove the pre-eminent home of the London department store. John Lewis sited a large store there in 1864, though it was the American Gordon Selfridge who transformed the street's possibilities when he opened his famous store at the unfashionable Marble Arch end in 1909. Others came too – Marshall and Snellgrove (now Debenhams), Marks and Spencer, DH Evans (now House of Fraser) and more. By then the department store had spread far and wide. It included its most famous presence of all – Harrod's, begun in Knightsbridge as Charles Harrod's family grocery in 1849, but grown by the twentieth century into one of the best-known stores in the world.

Shopping in London could never afford to rest on its laurels. From the 1970s, the concept of giant suburban shopping centres accessed by car had begun to take on from America. The biggest was the first, Brent Cross in north-west London, opened in 1976 and expanded since. It was followed by other "shopping cities" to all points of the London compass. They have since been dwarfed by "out-of-town" versions around the M25 orbital road, but they still serve a function in the full spectrum of the London shopping experience, incorporating global brands at one end, small independent characterful traders at the other and designer chic somewhere in between. Indeed, by the twenty-first century, London and shopping had become interchangeable concepts.

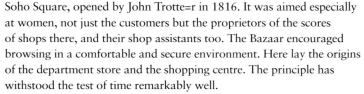

OPPOSITE The exterior of the old Covent Garden market, with market porters in the foreground. The market, which supplied Londoners with fresh fruit and vegetables, moved out to Nine Elms and the buildings were converted to shops and restaurants in the late 1970s and early 1980s. It is now a thriving area, popular with visitors to London, and a good example of successful inner city regeneration.

ABOVE A bold view of the Quadrant, Regent Street, with a red omnibus advertising Dewar's whisky in the foreground. The Quadrant is a section of the southern curve of Regent Street just north of Piccadilly Circus. This view shows it around 1920, just before the curved terrace was replaced by a similar but grander version. The rebuilt Regent Street was opened in 1927. The architect John Nash designed the original buildings, seen here, in the 1820s. The original colonnade was removed in 1852. Regent Street was already a major West End shopping street and this section included some of London's top men's tailoring shops: Dunn's, Austin Reed and Aquascutum.

BELOW Harrod's at night. Any visitor to London is usually familiar with the name of Harrod's, if not how to find it, and few pass up the opportunity to visit this legendary department store. At night the building is lit up, year round, providing an unmissable reminder of its existence on Brompton Road.

For Richer, for Poorer

LONDON, for much of its recent history the richest city on earth, has never been without its poor. They left little historical record of their existence in the earliest centuries, but official records from the medieval period tell of nuisances from beggars and the city authorities' efforts to curb them. Beggars were feared for many reasons. They carried disease, they stole to satisfy their needs, and they were ready contenders in any street disturbance, whatever its cause. Fear of their increasing numbers and unruly behaviour provoked volumes of laws (certainly from 1359 onwards, and no doubt before) which attempted to control vagrants and "sturdy" (threatening and workshy) beggars.

Beggars shared the London streets with another army. Prostitution was one more emblem of the city's intractable social problems. Not all street prostitutes were poor, but a great many were, or were on the verge of it. As with the beggars, no one could number them, though that did not stop clergymen and others coming up with wild estimates. Until education and job opportunities improved for women in the twentieth century, and sexual mores underwent a major shift from the 1960s, street prostitution continued to be a problem in London, and in some areas it still is today.

MESSRS. FRY AND FITCH'S

Southwark Female Farmed Poor House,

HARROW STREET, LANT STREET, BOROUGH.

BILL OF FARE.

Monday, ... 14 Ounces of Bread and 2 Ounces of Butter.

Tuesday, ... 14 Ounces of Bread, 6 Ounces of Meat when dressed, with Vegetables, and Broth for Supper.

Wednesday, ... 14 Ounces of Bread and 2 Ounces of Butter.

Thursday, ... 14 Ounces of Bread, 6 Ounces of Meat when dressed, with Vegetables, and Broth for Supper.

Friday, ... 14 Ounces of Bread and 2 Ounces of Butter.

Saturday, ... 14 Ounces of Bread, Pea Soup, and 1 Ounce of Butter, or 2 Ounces of Cheese for Supper.

Sunday, ... 14 Ounces of Bread, 6 Ounces of Meat when dressed, with Vegetables, and Broth for Supper.

Gruel for Breakfast every Morning.

Hot Water supplied for Tea, 6 Months in the year, in the Morning.

Pint and a Half of Table Beer each per day.

Mutton or Pork every other Sunday.

Easter, Whit, and Christmas Days, Mutton with Plum Pudding, and in the Season Green Peas or Beans, with good Bacon or Pork.

The whole of the above Articles to be of the best Quality.

And each Child as much as they ought reasonable to Eat and Drink, 3 times per Day.

For each Person, including Washing and Medical Attendance, at per Week. 4/6 –

Lying-in Women, with no other Charge for the 4 Weeks,

N. B. CLOTHING SUPPLIED ON MODERATE TERMS.

ABOVE A bill of fare from Fry and Fitch's Female Farmed Poor House in Harrow Street, Southwark, around 1830. It offered to keep paupers at a cheap rate, taking girls in for 4s 6d (22.5 pence) a week, or only around £25 at today's prices.

OPPOSITE Between 1886 and 1903 the sociologist Charles Booth studied working-class London. He drew up maps colouring each street according to the class of its occupants. Red marked the well-to-do and black the "semi-criminal and degraded".

LEFT The "Crawlers". This destitute woman is caring for the child of a friend working in a coffee shop nearby – the child "cried and wheezed and coughed" as the photograph was taken, around 1877.

WEALTHY

WELL-TO-DO

COMFORTABLE

POOR & COMFORTABLE (MIXED)

POOR

VERY POOR

SEMI-CRIMINAL

Public Pleasures

Public spectacle has been an important part of London life from the very beginning. The entry of Roman governors into London, their displays at the amphitheatre to show off the spoils of war and to test the strength of gladiators began a long tradition of Londoners' delight in colour, glamour, noise and show. Almost any event could provide an excuse for a public party. Declarations of war in medieval times would be proclaimed by royal heralds at different points in the town, witnessed by huge crowds. Demonstrations on the occasions of victories or peace treaties would call for the illumination of every house that could afford candles and oil lamps, with huge fireworks displays in the parks and on the river.

Each year was also punctuated by the London fairs which provided their own brand of colourful spectacle – May Fair, Southwark Fair and, most famous of all, Bartholomew (or Bartlemy) Fair. Held at Smithfield at the end of August, from at least 1133, Bartlemy was a great gathering of buyers and sellers of food, clothes and household goods, together with acrobats, jugglers, puppeteers, monsters, menageries and every exotic under the sun. It was a scene of riotous fun, sometimes just plain riot. Even the Puritans could not suppress it, but eventually it faded away and was proclaimed for the last time in 1855. It had lasted, one of the great popular institutions of London, for over seven centuries.

Smithfield was a great open space but the "lungs" of London were its parks, and Hyde Park was the greatest of all. It had long been a deer park for royalty before being opened to the public in the 1630s and walled round as parkland in the 1660s. St James's Park was in use from about the same time, the Green Park somewhat later. As London grew, it became important to preserve green space from development, and so philanthropists and local councils bought up farms and gardens of great mansions near London, and endowed them for use as open space in perpetuity. One of the greatest of these initiatives was Victoria Park in Hackney, laid out for the use of east-enders from 1842. It had lakes for boating and bathing, a bandstand, cricket and football pitches and a gymnasium. But it was not solely a place of recreation. Huge political meetings were often held there and it was a centre, like Hyde Park, for Sunday "spouters" and oratorical cranks of all denominations.

Besides the parks, some private open spaces were devoted to the profitable pursuit of pleasure. One of the earliest was Spring Gardens, south of where Trafalgar Square now stands. It was laid out around

BELOW A bird's-eye perspective of Vauxhall Gardens around 1750. The bandstand or "Orchestra" is in the centre and the supper boxes in loggias around the edges.

1610 for bowling greens, shady walks, and facilities for taking the clear spring water to be found there. Water, though, was not enough, and the pleasure gardens soon became notorious for wine, women and song. The eighteenth century saw their heyday, with a palace of pleasure at Ranelagh Gardens, Chelsea, for aristocrats and the rich and famous, where concerts and masked balls were held through the summer; and a slightly more down-market affair at Vauxhall Gardens, infamous for its expensive sandwiches made from transparently thin ham. Vauxhall Gardens survived into the second half of the nineteenth century, and was rivalled by Cremorne Gardens on the other side of the river at Chelsea. Both had their decidedly seamy side. After 10 p.m., the respectable visitors left and the Gardens would be populated by prostitutes and those who had come to be tempted, or just to watch the antics.

In London's recent history there have been some very special events which have drawn the eyes of the nation, sometimes of the world, to London. The Great Exhibition of 1851 was the first and one of the biggest. In the Crystal Palace, a giant greenhouse erected in Hyde Park, 6.2 million people paid to see the manufactures and artefacts of the world brought to London and put on vast public display. Everyone visited, from the Royal Family to the poorest rural labourer. Afterwards, the Crystal Palace was sold and re-erected on a larger scale in Sydenham, south-east London, as a concert-hall and visitor attraction until it burned down in 1936. There were other exhibitions, notably in 1862, 1908 and 1924, and then the Festival of Britain in 1951. The Festival aimed to recreate something of the excitement of the Great Exhibition to lighten the gloom of post-war London. It was a great success, and left the Royal Festival Hall to be enjoyed by Londoners ever since.

See also facsimile item 11 in envelope 3, opposite page 64.

FUN ON THE ICE

In 1173, William FitzStephen recorded that "When the great marsh which washes the northern walls of the city freezes, crowds of young men go out to play on the ice. Some of them fit shinbones of cattle on their feet, tying them round their ankles. They take a stick with an iron spike in the hands and strike it regularly on the ice, and are carried along as fast as a flying bird or a bolt from a catapult." They wore polished bone skates like these (below), which date from around 1200, though the leather strap is a later addition. Skating proved an enduring winter pastime in London, though it could be risky. In January 1867, the ice broke on Regent's Park lake plunging 200 skaters into the water; 40 died, mostly local young men "apparently in the middle class of life".

RIGHT An aquatint depicting Bartholomew Fair in 1721. The richly dressed figure on the right is Prime Minister Sir Robert Walpole among food-stalls, theatre booths, street-sellers, acrobats, beggars and visitors.

Stage and Screen

In the early days, theatre in London took place in the open. Medieval Mystery Plays were recorded in London from 1173. They represented scripture to the masses on festival days and took place on "scaffolds" or open-air stages, and were sometimes performed over several days, as by the parish clerks at Clerkenwell in the 1390s. Stage performance was also a feature of the great London fairs – St Bartholomew's Fair at Smithfield, and Southwark Fair in Borough High Street had theatrical booths with skilled actors well into the eighteenth century. Players would come out of the London playhouses to perform before ragged but appreciative crowds. Playwrights wrote "drolls" or comedy sketches specially for each season. And Richardson's theatrical booth was the chief draw at Bartlemy around 1800 with plays like *Monk and Murder; Or, The Skeleton Spectre*.

By then, though, London had become the home of the theatre as modern audiences know it. James Burbadge's Theatre – that was its name, revealing the uniqueness of the venture – was the first of the purpose-built structures to house drama in London. It was put up in Shoreditch in 1576. The Curtain was opened nearby a year later, in which a young actor called William Shakespeare trod the boards. In 1598, the Theatre was dismantled and rebuilt south of the river on Bankside, this time as the Globe: it joined the Swan, opened there two years before. Another, this time in the City and called the Rose, was a few years older. This great flourishing of the "Renaissance Theatre" would have its setbacks. The Globe burned down in 1613, the fate of so many theatres that relied on candle or oil power to keep them lit.

The Puritans closed the London theatres from 1642, but they revived with the restoration of the monarchy under Charles II. The Theatre Royal, Drury Lane – opened in 1663 – is the oldest theatre in London to occupy the same site continuously, though the building itself has gone through many transformations. Others followed, including an Opera House in the Haymarket. Most famous of all, the Theatre Royal Covent Garden, was opened at Christmas 1732 by the impresario John Rich. London theatre throve throughout the eighteenth century, especially Drury Lane under David Garrick, the most charismatic actor of his day. Garrick strove to maintain an interest in serious drama, but audiences thirsted for spectacle and variety above all.

Garrick and Rich were the beginning of the West End theatre industry. London's "West End" and "theatre" remain synonymous for many visitors to this day. By the twenty-first century, there were 51 West End theatres and a further 48 in other parts of London, including the South Bank (with the reconstructed Globe and the National Theatre). This was the most vibrant "Theatreland" in the world. Shakespeare, who was there almost from the beginning, still continued to play a leading part.

LEFT Southwark Fair, pictured by William Hogarth in 1733–34. It was a popular venue for travelling theatres and here we see the stage collapsing under Colley Cibber, the Poet Laureate, a favourite butt of contemporary wits.

OPPOSITE TOP Theatre Royal, Drury Lane, around 1808. The first theatre on this site dated from 1663 but burned down. So did this one, in 1809 – just after this view of its sumptuous interior was made.

OPPOSITE BOTTOM Theatreland. Shaftesbury Avenue at night, around the turn of the twenty-first century. There were then some 167 theatre venues in London, one of the city's great draws for tourists from around the world.

Through all this, variety stayed close to the heart of the Londoner. That passion spawned a special "Theatre of Varieties" – the Music Hall. Developed in the "long rooms" built on to public houses as places of entertainment, a popular theatre of song, chorus dancing, comedy acts, clowns, magicians and acrobats developed into the true expression of cockney pleasure. The first purpose-built music hall seems to have been the Canterbury, opened on Westminster Bridge Road in 1852. It was a grand place for its day, but it had nothing to match the luxury and splendour of the later music halls of the 1890s, especially the Alhambra and the Empire, both in Leicester Square.

These in their turn were eclipsed by the Picture Palace. The cinema rose out of the music hall, with moving pictures just another attraction in the variety show on offer in the 1890s. "The flicks" took off with a vengeance. The music hall offered fantasy and escapism of a sort, but the cinema transported its audiences to entirely different worlds. By 1914, many places in London showed just film alone. But it was from 1930, and the arrival of "the talkies", that cinema in London became a life-shaping craze for a large

CHAMPAGNES

	BOTT.	½ BOTT.
VAUBAN FRERES, SPECIAL CUVEE	8/-	4/6
ST. MARCEAUX, FIRST QUALITY	10/6	5/6
WACHTER, ROYAL CHARTER	10/6	5/6
IRROY, CARTE D'OR	10/6	5/6
G. H. MUMM, EXTRA QUALITY	10/6	5/6
MONTEBELLO, MAXIMUM SEC	10/6	5/6
MOET, DRY IMPERIAL	10/6	5/6
DELBECK, EXTRA RESERVE	10/6	5/6
HEIDSICK, DRY MONOPOLE	11/6	6/-
L. ROEDERER, EXTRA DRY	11/6	6/-
VEUVE CLICQUOT, DRY	11/6	6/-
POMMERY, EXTRA SEC	11/6	6/-

Fine Old Vintage Wines. See Special Wine List.

MINERAL WATERS + BOTTLED BEERS

	Lge.	Small.
LEMONADE, SELTZER AND SODA	4d.	2d.
SCHWEPPE'S SODA	6d.	—
JOHANNIS AND APOLLINARIS	1/-	6d.

	Bot.	Pt.		Bot.	Pt.
BASS'S PALE ALE	1/-	6d.	SCOTCH ALE	1/-	6d.
GUINNESS'S STOUT	1/-	6d.	PILSENER LAGER BEER	1/-	6d.

BASS'S FINEST BITTER ALE AND STOUT .... PER GLASS.
.... 2d.

THE ROYAL

HOLBORN

THEATRE OF VARIETIES

Prices of Admission

PRIVATE BOXES	10s 6 TO £2:2
FAUTEUILS	3 s.
STALLS	2 s.
BALCONY	1 s.
AREA	6 d.

PROGRAMME 2d

Mr. JOAN BRILL, PROPRIETOR

Mr. GEO. BURGESS, MANAGER

proportion of Londoners. The great chains of Astorias and Empires revolutionized entertainment for the mass of the people. Luxurious exotic surroundings (Egyptian décor was a favourite of the times), pile carpets, central heating, yielding armchairs, all was utterly alien to the living conditions of most Londoners at the time. And the on-screen experience, from Hollywood to Robin Hood, transported everyone from their daily lives, however humdrum. Cinema continued to be the most popular mass entertainment until television arrived to provide Londoners with escapism at home.

LEFT A programme from 1900 for the Royal Holborn Theatre of Varieties (the Holborn Empire). Typical of classic London music hall in its heyday, the artists included the comedienne Vesta Victoria (of "Daddy Wouldn't Buy Me a Bow-Wow" fame).

RIGHT Joseph (or Joe) Grimaldi (1778–1837), the foremost pantomime artist of his day and best known for his work as a clown at Sadler's Wells Theatre from 1800. His memoirs were edited by Charles Dickens, a great admirer.

BELOW RIGHT The Astoria Cinema at Finsbury Park was among many "super-cinemas" bringing a new dimension of luxury to a night out in London. It opened in 1930, had a Spanish Garden and Rotunda Fountain Court, and seated over 3,000 people.

J. GRIMALDI as CLOWN.
at Sadler's Wells Theatre

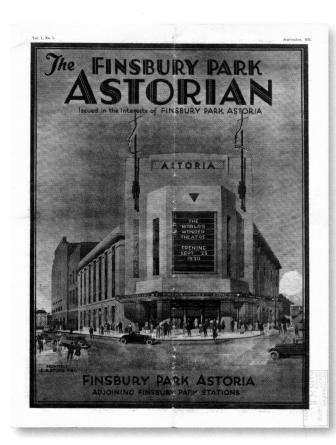

The FINSBURY PARK
ASTORIAN
Issued in the Interests of FINSBURY PARK ASTORIA

ASTORIA

THE WORLD'S WONDER THEATRE
OPENING SEPT 29 1930

FINSBURY PARK ASTORIA
ADJOINING FINSBURY PARK STATIONS

Sporting London

When it comes to sport, the world owes London a lot. Sport has been here from time immemorial. There have been games of strength (wrestling, tug-of-war), of speed and stamina (sprinting and long-distance running), of skill (archery, skittles, bowls), and quickness of eye (ball games with hand, foot, and bat). Even in the 1100s, we read of football, a brutal sport in which men could be killed, and of something like cricket two centuries later. Real tennis was a favourite of the Tudors and so was bowls. All had their London venues.

But the capacity to enjoy sport, as spectator or competitor, depended upon spare time, and this in turn relied on relative prosperity. As this increased, so did the diversity of sports on offer. Eighteenth-century London, for instance, was a place of sporting innovation. Horseracing, boxing and cricket had their present-day origins then. All were associated with the greatest craze of the age – gambling. All were London sports, patronized by West End aristocrats and moneyed men, as well as plebeian audiences.

They took place most frequently in the villages and open spaces around London. Sometimes London would move out to envelop these sporting venues. So Thomas Lord's cricket ground in Marylebone, opened in 1787, was first built over and then, when it reopened in St John's Wood in 1814, built all around. Lord's is, of course, the "Home of Cricket", but other world sports have their homes in London too.

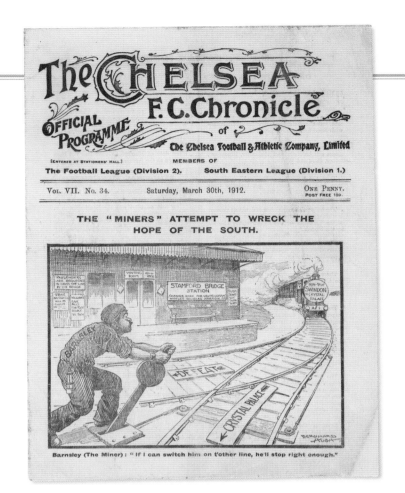

ABOVE London's football clubs have some of the longest and proudest histories of any in the world. Here is an early number of a fans' magazine, *The Chelsea F.C. Chronicle*, from 1912.

LEFT Rat-catching at the Blue Anchor Tavern, Bunhill Row, Finsbury, around 1849. A terrier called Tiny the Wonder (from Manchester) is shown killing 200 rats in under an hour for a fat wager.

OPPOSITE A scorecard for a cricket match between the Gentlemen of England and the touring Australian team at Kennington Oval in June 1884. The Australians won, but lost the Test series later that summer.

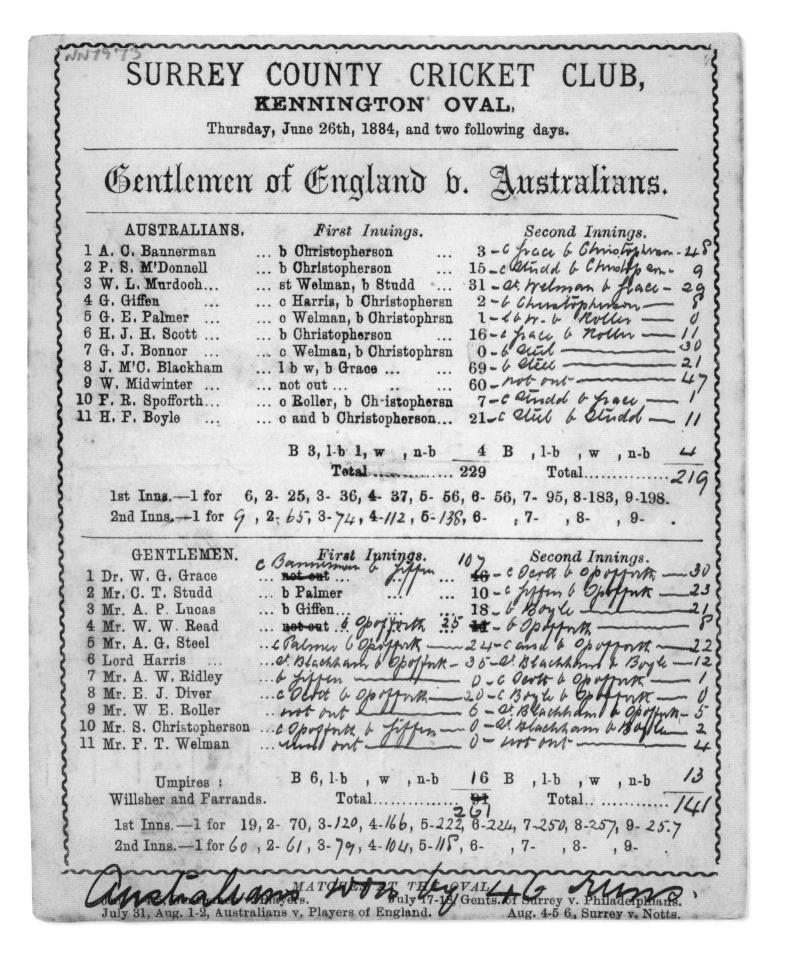

SURREY COUNTY CRICKET CLUB,
KENNINGTON OVAL,
Thursday, June 26th, 1884, and two following days.

Gentlemen of England b. Australians.

AUSTRALIANS.	First Innings.		Second Innings.	
1 A. C. Bannerman	... b Christopherson	...	3 — c Grace b Christopherson	48
2 P. S. M'Donnell	... b Christopherson	...	15 — c Studd b Christopherson	9
3 W. L. Murdoch	... st Welman, b Studd	...	31 — st Welman b Grace	29
4 G. Giffen	... c Harris, b Christophersn		2 — b Christopherson	8
5 G. E. Palmer	... c Welman, b Christophrsn		1 — l b w. b Roller	0
6 H. J. H. Scott	... b Christopherson	...	16 — c Grace b Roller	11
7 G. J. Bonnor	... c Welman, b Christophrsn		0 — b Steel	30
8 J. M'C. Blackham	... l b w, b Grace	...	69 — b Steel	21
9 W. Midwinter	... not out	...	60 — not out	47
10 F. R. Spofforth	... c Roller, b Christophersn		7 — c Studd b Grace	1
11 H. F. Boyle	... c and b Christopherson	...	21 — c Studd b Studd	11

B 3, l-b 1, w , n-b   4   B , l-b , w , n-b   4

Total.............. 229   Total................ 219

1st Inns.—1 for 6, 2- 25, 3- 36, 4- 37, 5- 56, 6- 56, 7- 95, 8-183, 9-198.

2nd Inns.—1 for 9 , 2- 65, 3- 74, 4-112, 5-138, 6- , 7- , 8- , 9- .

GENTLEMEN.	First Innings.		Second Innings.	
1 Dr. W. G. Grace	c Bannerman b Giffen 107 not out	46	c Scott b Spofforth	30
2 Mr. C. T. Studd	... b Palmer	10	c Giffen b Spofforth	23
3 Mr. A. P. Lucas	... b Giffen	18	b Boyle	21
4 Mr. W. W. Read	not out b Spofforth 35	11	b Spofforth	8
5 Mr. A. G. Steel	c Palmer b Spofforth	24	c and b Spofforth	22
6 Lord Harris	st Blackham b Spofforth	35	st Blackham b Boyle	12
7 Mr. A. W. Ridley	b Giffen	0	c Scott b Spofforth	1
8 Mr. E. J. Diver	c Scott b Spofforth	20	c Boyle b Spofforth	0
9 Mr. W. E. Roller	not out	6	st Blackham b Spofforth	5
10 Mr. S. Christopherson	c Spofforth b Giffen	0	st Blackham b Boyle	2
11 Mr. F. T. Welman	shut out	0	not out	4

Umpires :   B 6, l-b , w , n-b   16   B , l-b , w , n-b   13

Willsher and Farrands.   Total.............. 261   Total............. 141

1st Inns.—1 for 19, 2- 70, 3-120, 4-166, 5-222, 6-224, 7-250, 8-257, 9- 257.

2nd Inns.—1 for 60 , 2- 61, 3- 79, 4-104, 5-115, 6- , 7- , 8- , 9- .

Australians won by 46 runs.

MATCHES AT THE OVAL.

v. Players.   July 17-18, Gents. of Surrey v. Philadelphians.
July 31, Aug. 1-2, Australians v. Players of England.   Aug. 4-5 6, Surrey v. Notts.

Most important of all, the Football Association was formed at a meeting in the Freemason's Tavern, near Lincoln's Inn Fields, in October 1863; it was there that the definitive rules of the game were established. Within a decade or two, with the leisure capacity of the skilled working class expanding, football became a truly popular sport. Hackney Marshes accommodated the largest collection of football pitches in the world. More prestigious grounds and clubs would emerge. Fulham Football Club dates from 1879, Tottenham Hotspur from 1882, Arsenal 1886, West Ham 1895, and Chelsea from 1905. Wembley Stadium, built for the British Empire Exhibition of 1924, was opened in 1923. The FA Cup Final that year attracted some 250,000 spectators; so many, that for a time the pitch was filled with them. The rebuilt stadium remains, for many, the Home of Football.

ABOVE Wimbledon, home of world tennis for over 130 years, pictured during the Wimbledon Lawn Tennis Championships of 2008. The Wimbledon fortnight remains the premier event in the international tennis calendar.

In like manner Wimbledon is the Home of Tennis. The All England Club, which first determined the rules of tennis, was established there in 1868. The first tennis championship was held at Wimbledon in 1877 and became an international affair around 1900. Across the river, Twickenham is the Home of Rugby Union Football, and the rugby stadium opened there in 1907. The river itself has played host to the Universities Boat Race between Putney and Mortlake annually since 1856. And another great sporting event firmly established a home in London from 1981: the London Marathon.

No other city in the world can claim such an influential heritage in helping the world fill its leisure hours. London will have been home to the Olympics three times, in 1908, 1948, and 2012. No other city has hosted more than two games in the era of the modern Olympics. It is fitting that, as the best established of world cities, London should have been the favourite choice for the greatest assembly of human endeavour known to mankind.

A special stadium was built for the Olympics of 1908 at White City in West London. It held 150,000 spectators, most of them standing. Perhaps the most memorable moment of the games was when the Italian marathon runner Dorando Pietri collapsed shortly before the line and was assisted to the finish by officials. Though awarded the medal, he was later disqualified, but he won the crowd's hearts in the process.

The 1948 Olympics were the first to be held after a disastrous war. The city's resources were so stretched that it could hardly put food on Londoners' plates. Even so, the "Austerity Games" were a huge success. Of many memorable achievements, the 17-year old American Bob Mathias won the decathlon – he remains to this day the youngest winner of a men's athletic event.

London was declared the winner of the 2012 games bid on July 6, 2005. The city's joy was tempered by the terrible events of the next day (see p.42). But everyone was confident that the games themselves would showcase the triumph of human endeavour over adversity: a fitting symbol for the times.

See also facsimile item 12 in envelope 3, opposite page 64.

OVERLEAF The London 2012 Olympic site showing the completion of the main stadium's shell in June 2009. It was just one element in a project of almost fantastic complexity and enormous cost, intended to transform the face of East London.

BELOW The 153rd Oxford and Cambridge Boat Race in April 2007, in which Cambridge were the victors. Many London sporting events have a very long history and this is no exception.

OLYMPIC CITY

London has the honour of being the first city to host three Olympics in the modern Olympiad, but one was very much by accident. Rome had been selected for 1908 but the eruption of Vesuvius in 1906 made Italy's first priority the rebuilding of Naples. London's White City Stadium was built in just 10 months, and opened when the games began in April 1908. Twenty-two nations took part and Great Britain swept the medals table, with 146 against the USA's 47 in second place. The 1948 Olympics showed how the balance of power in the sporting world had shifted: the USA came first with 84 medals and Britain came twelfth. The games also marked something like a return to international normality, attracting athletes from 59 nations, 14 (including Iraq) for the first time. Germany and Japan, still under Allied occupation, were barred from sending competitors.

ABOVE Two ticket stubs and an Olympic torch from the London Olympics of 1948. They were dubbed the Austerity Games, put on by a cash-strapped post-war nation.

From Purcell to Punk

London has a gloriously rich musical heritage. On the one hand, music has been performed daily at Westminster Abbey for nearly 950 years. On the other, the even older traditions of street music in London are kept alive by buskers in Covent Garden and elsewhere, their performances officially extended in recent years to Tube stations. Dancing in the streets to a barrel organ or other instruments lasted well into the first half of the twentieth century. In the 1930s, dancing was encouraged in the parks – 20,000 danced to a band in Highbury Fields shortly before the Second World War – and it remains one of London's great diversions, as the city's nightclubs and dance-halls have testified, particularly since the 1920s.

Henry Purcell, born in Westminster, was the first great London composer of the modern era, dying in 1695. But it was the next century that witnessed London's musical flowering. George Frederick Handel left his native Germany to come to London at the age of 25 in 1710. He would spend most of the remainder of his days there, becoming an English citizen in 1727 and dying at his house in Brook Street, Mayfair, in 1759. The Handel years were among the very greatest in London's long musical history. Most famously, in July 1717 Handel performed his *Water Music* to accompany the royal barge on journeys down the Thames; and in April 1749, his *Music for the Royal Fireworks* was played at an elaborate celebration in Green Park to mark a peace with France. Handel established London as an international magnet for musical performers. Thomas Arne, JC Bach ("the London Bach"), Mozart

and Haydn all performed their works in one of Europe's great musical capitals.

Nineteenth-century London would not prove as fruitful musically but there were innovations nonetheless. Music in the home was livelier than ever before – London's Camden Town was the home of piano making in Britain. Gilbert and Sullivan brought comic operetta to the London stage from 1871, and later had a home of their own at the Savoy Theatre, Strand. Then, in August 1895, at Queen's Hall, began the Promenade Concerts, or Proms. Later to run daily for six weeks every summer, the Proms moved to the Royal Albert Hall in 1942. There they quickly established themselves as the greatest classical music festival in the world.

London also featured as a subject in music, especially in popular song. Famous locales such as Berkeley Square, Lambeth, the Old Kent Road, Leicester Square, the Strand, Waterloo and many more appeared in songs right through the twentieth century. There are more than 120 songs with London in the title, and hundreds more are set there. But it was from the 1950s in particular that the musical identity of London underwent a revolution. The influence of American rock music on London audiences and musicians was revelatory. Tommy Steele, a singer from Bermondsey, became one of the best-loved performers of the age, his venue the 2i's Coffee-Bar in Soho. Skiffle, a home-grown café music, made an international star of Lonnie Donegan, brought up in East Ham. And in those same years further developments were strongly influenced by new migrants to London from the Caribbean.

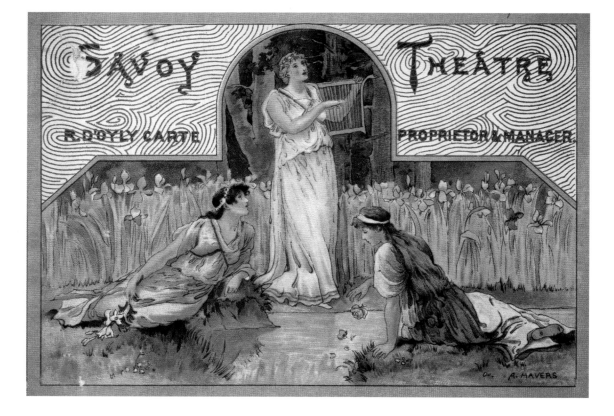

LEFT The cover of a programme for *The Mikado* at the Savoy Theatre in 1885. Sullivan's catchy music and Gilbert's witty libretto proved a winning combination throughout their long career from 1871 to 1896.

BELOW The peace ending Britain's war with France and Spain was celebrated in April 1749 with a huge firework display in Green Park, accompanied by a great Handel celebration set piece, *Music for the Royal Fireworks*.

BUSKING IT

Street music has been a feature of London life for centuries. In the fourteenth century, the minstrel accompanying himself on a harp was a feature of fairs, and fiddlers were welcomed in pubs, or played to dancers in the streets. The nineteenth century saw a particularly rich flowering of street music, and it is around 1850 that the words "busking" and "busker" first find their way into print. The German band, an especially tuneless brand of street music, more blackmail than entertainment, appeared around that time. But it was the Italians who were most associated with the barrel organ shown here, made around 1900. This one was built by Pasquale & Co, of Phoenix Place, in the heart of Holborn's Italian quarter. The tune was made by a holed cylinder which the organ-grinder turned by a crank – "music by Handle", as the wits called it.

The Sixties and Liverpool will always be linked in the pop music of the time. But London was not far behind. The Rolling Stones hailed from Gravesend, just downriver from London. The Kinks were from north London, Adam Faith from Acton, The Who from Shepherds Bush, Cream from Chelsea, Queen from west London, David Bowie from Brixton, Marc Bolan and T-Rex from Hackney. In the 1970s, Johnny Rotten, Sid Vicious and the Sex Pistols hailed from north London, Madness from Camden Town, and The Clash from Notting Hill: their great hit *London Calling* was released in 1979.

By then, London had become a massive venue for popular music. The pub, perhaps London's most versatile institution, became a popular venue for rock music, especially punk in the 1970s and 1980s. Pubs like the Hope & Anchor in Islington and the Red Cow in Hammersmith achieved national renown. And when rock music moved into the city's great open spaces the whole world took notice. Hyde Park was first used as a rock venue in 1968 and Wembley Stadium in 1972 – Live Aid had its British venue there in July 1985, playing to 82,000 people. Even the unpopular Millennium Dome in Greenwich reinvented itself as the O2 Stadium, becoming quickly famous for its extravagant gigs. By the twenty-first century London could justly claim to be music capital of the world.

OPPOSITE TOP LEFT Rock as a world force, mobilizing resources for Africa at Live Aid in Wembley Stadium, July 13, 1985. Bob Geldof and Midge Ure were the main organizers.

OPPOSITE TOP RIGHT Punk style and music became very much a London phenomenon from the mid-1970s. The fashion designer Vivienne Westwood, who studied art in London, is in the plaid suit on the right in 1977.

OPPOSITE BOTTOM The BBC Proms are the world's greatest music festival. The traditional celebratory "Last Night of the Proms" rounds off each festival, as here in 2008.

BOTTOM LEFT The song sheet of "I Don't Like London", sung around 1900 by T.W. Barrett, a comical singer of the music halls. Songs for performance at home had a massive sale from the 1870s on.

BOTTOM RIGHT A song sheet for George Leybourne's popular song celebrating the telegraph, around 1865. Born in Newcastle, Leybourne was also known as "Champagne Charlie".

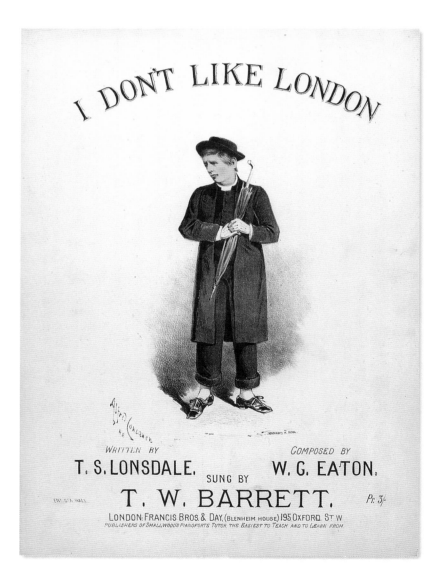

Meat and Drink

THE London public house is a timeless institution. Its early history is obscure, but perhaps the Tabard Inn in Borough High Street, Southwark, might stand as the father of them all. It opened in the early 1300s, and it was here that Geoffrey Chaucer assembled his storytellers before their pilgrimage in his Canterbury Tales, written around 1388. The Boar's Head Tavern in Eastcheap was Falstaff's favourite hostelry, put on the stage by Shakespeare in the 1590s. The famous Ye Olde Cheshire Cheese, still standing in Fleet Street, has been there since 1667, its predecessor having burned down in the Great Fire: a pub has been on the site since 1538 and probably for centuries before that.

From the 1650s, the public house competed for custom with a new institution, the coffee house, which sold wines and spirits as well as coffee but was dedicated as much to business as to pleasure. Coffee houses were especially – though by no means entirely – a City institution and many developed a specialist clientele: West India merchants at the Jamaica, stock-brokers and jobbers at Jonathan's (where the London Stock Exchange began), and insurers and ships' captains at Lloyd's. Others were less respectable: some coffee houses were little more than brothels. Both pub and coffee house became the venue for social gatherings of men with common political and leisure interests too. The London club had its beginnings in the eighteenth century in such gatherings. By the 1820s and '30s, rising prosperity allowed better-off club members to build premises for their exclusive use: the great London Clubs of Pall Mall and St James's date from those years.

Drink was not always so convivial, however. Gin was a fiery spirit of Dutch origin that became all the rage among poorer Londoners. The 1730s was the decade of the "Gin Craze". Gin-fuelled oblivion was the quickest way out of squalor and hunger. It was cheap, and a nip could be had not just at pubs but at every grocer's or chandler's in the capital. Some of it was brewed in backyards and proved deadly. "Blue ruin", just one of its nicknames, came from the cornflower-blue complexion that some addicts developed. Attempts by Parliament to control its sale from 1736 proved of limited success: rising prosperity and improved living standards among London's "lower orders" probably did more to break the habit than force of law.

The term "Gin Palace", as the luxurious London pubs of the 1820s were known, indicates that gin remained a favourite tipple. But these palaces – with their engraved plate-glass windows, polished brass-work, brilliant gas-lighting, welcoming coal-fires, mahogany interiors and carpeted floors – sold much else besides. In the Victorian period – probably the London pub's finest hour – they became the favourite resort of Londoners starved of comfort in their own homes. There would be even greater luxury in the hotels that sprung up around the railway termini from the 1830s on (the Great Northern at King's Cross, the Great Eastern at Liverpool Street, the magnificent Midland Grand Hotel at St Pancras and many more). These were joined in the last quarter of the century by other superb hotels in many of London's main streets.

ABOVE A stone sign of a boar's head, dated 1668, from a tavern in Eastcheap in the City of London. Wooden signs were more common until their general removal from London streets in the 1760s.

RIGHT The cobbled courtyard and medieval galleries of the old Tabard Inn, Borough High Street, in 1870, captured by the watercolourist Louise Rayner not long before its demolition in 1873.

THE MODERN PLAGUE OF LONDON

SHOWING THE PUBLIC HOUSES AS SPECIFIED IN THE LONDON DIR

EXCLUSIVE OF LICENSED HOTELS, GROCERS, &c. &c.

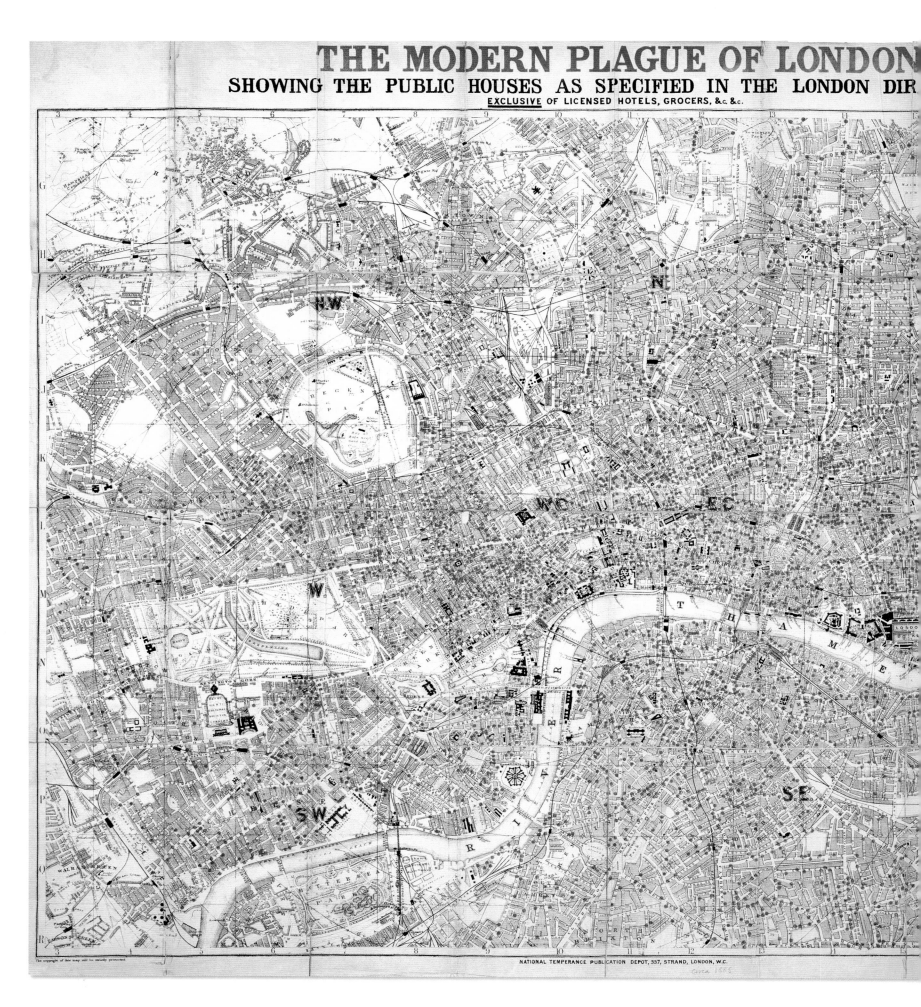

NATIONAL TEMPERANCE PUBLICATION DEPOT, 337, STRAND, LONDON, W.C.

LEFT AND BELOW The Modern Plague of London, published by the National Temperance League in 1886, showing the ubiquitous temptations from drink at London's myriad public houses. Pubs catered for all classes below the very wealthy and were popular among women as well as men. The blown-up section shows the cluster of pubs for theatregoers and pleasure-seekers in the West End, the lawyers' watering holes around Chancery Lane, and the workers' pubs near Smithfield.

A City chop house captured by Thomas Rowlandson around 1812. Known as "slap-bangs" for their swift service, diners were not encouraged to linger, though the eager waiter expected a halfpenny or penny tip for his trouble.

Side-by-side with the great hotels were great restaurants. Sometimes, as at the Savoy, they shared the same premises. Indeed, eating out had often been an accompaniment to drinking in inns and taverns and for centuries, the London taverns were the city's restaurants and great dining halls. Tentatively in the eighteenth century, and more aggressively in the nineteenth, specialist restaurants established themselves. Many of the first and best were French and located in Soho, where many French migrants had their home. Where the French led, others followed. By the 1930s, guides to eating out in London listed French, Italian, German, Jewish, Hungarian and Spanish restaurants. There were Indian restaurants near Euston Station and Chinese in Limehouse. People from the Caribbean and Africa from the late-1940s brought yet more variety. But it was the 1970s, with increased migration, especially from the Middle East and the Indian Sub-Continent, which changed the eating habits of the Londoner for ever. By the end of the twentieth century, after further arrivals from Eastern Europe in particular, it was possible to eat one's way round the world not just in famously cosmopolitan areas like Soho or the East End, but in every high street in London: Stoke Newington Church Street, say, or Upper Street, Islington. And one of the most famous dishes to emerge from this gastronomic expansion was the Londoner's favourite dish – chicken tikka masala.
See also facsimile item 13 in envelope 3, opposite page 64.

ABOVE An eel and pie shop around 1928. Stewed eels, and pie and mash with green liquor (parsley sauce) were the staple fare. A few such establishments remain in inner London.

ABOVE RIGHT The East and West Chinese Restaurant in Limehouse, photographed by Henry Grant in 1955. The world's cuisines gradually began to fascinate the Londoner as post-war immigration dropped off.

RIGHT Claridge's Hotel lighting up for Christmas. Hotels and fine dining have been a notable feature of London life since the nineteenth century, Claridge's dating from the 1850s.

Health and Hospitals

THE oldest surviving hospital in Britain, St Bartholomew's at Smithfield, seems to have originated in an act of charity by one man, Rahere, a favourite of Henry I. He founded his hospital for the sick poor in 1123. Many of the other early hospitals originated in the religious houses of London. St Thomas's Hospital was founded within a Southwark priory in the 1170s. And the Priory of St Mary Bethlehem in Bishopsgate began to house the sick from around 1330 – it was the beginning of the Bethlem Hospital or Bedlam. In the late medieval period, London could boast around 30 hospitals and almshouses for the aged poor. By this time, rich City merchants and their livery companies had also begun to share in the burden of caring for the sick.

At the end of the seventeenth century, the nation was shamed by the example of France into caring for its injured warriors. The Royal Military Hospital at Chelsea, from 1682, and the Royal Naval Hospital at Greenwich, from 1694, were both designed by Christopher Wren. But it was the period from 1720 to 1760 that saw the greatest period of general-hospital building in London's history. They were all charitable ventures, sometimes by one man (Thomas Guy who built

his hospital in Southwark from 1721), but more usually by public subscriptions led by City merchants and the nobility. The Westminster, St George's, the London and the Middlesex all had their beginnings in this period. The succeeding decades saw the arrival of many specialist hospitals, especially for smallpox and lying-in (childbirth).

The mentally ill had not been neglected in this innovative period: St Luke's Hospital opened in Old Street in 1751. It was near to the ancient Bethlem Hospital, which relocated to Moorfields on the northern edge of the City in 1675. Bedlam, as it was universally known, was one of "the lions" or great attractions of London in the eighteenth century. No journey to the capital was complete without it. For a few pennies, the keepers would show visitors the wards and every cell. Mad men and women were made a show for gawping rustics and sneering beaux alike. Such exhibitions were stopped around 1775, and the hospital relocated to Lambeth in 1815.

Hospital building continued in the nineteenth century but its institutions were less grandiose and funding came from the state rather than charity. The new Poor Law Act of 1834 paved the way for infirmaries for the sick poor; and fever hospitals were

LEFT A madhouse scene from *A Rake's Progress* by William Hogarth, 1735. It is probably Bedlam, one of the sights of London, where "lunatics" were shown to visitors for a fee.

BELOW John O'Connor, *The Embankment*, 1874. The Victoria Embankment, containing the northern interceptor sewer, was part of the greatest sanitary improvement of Victorian London.

MR GUY'S HOSPITAL

Before 1948, many of London's great hospitals were established and run as charities. Guy's Hospital, Southwark, was founded by Thomas Guy, a rich London printer. It took in its first patients in 1726, a year after its benefactor died. Maintaining this great hospital and its later medical school relied mainly on rents from Guy's bequeathed property, but by the late nineteenth century public appeals for donations had become increasingly necessary. In the 1920s, when this poster was published, Guy's and most other hospitals relied on flag days, fêtes, fairs, charity balls, bazaars, carnivals, ballroom-dancing competitions, concerts, exhibitions, sporting events, skywriting adverts and so on. Funding was at last put on a sounder footing, paid for by the taxpayer, when hospitals were taken over by the National Health Service in 1948.

Faiths of London

Religious tolerance was generally one of the pillars of the Roman Empire, and so the faiths of Londinium were legion. Many gods, Roman, Egyptian and more have left their images for the archaeologists to uncover. One of the greatest of all finds was the Temple of Mithras, dating from around 240 and dedicated to an eastern cult whose beliefs remain obscure, but which valued virtue, courage and honour. Typical of the Romans' hedging-one's-bets approach to religion, statues of other gods besides Mithras were found there.

Christianity would change all that. An early Christian community and bishop were based in London in the fourth century, but it was from 604, when Pope Gregory I's mission established a bishopric, that London would be a Christian city for the next 1,400 years and more. The first church to St Paul dates from this early period and there would be several before the Normans established their great cathedral on the same site from 1087. That took over 200 years to build, and underwent constant reconstruction until the fourteenth century. By then, St Paul's had been joined by a host of smaller parish churches. Their forest of towers and spires would dominate the London skyline for centuries

ABOVE The back of a fifteenth-century blue enamel and gold crucifix showing the Virgin and Child. The gold pin can be removed to reveal a sliver of the "True Cross".

RIGHT The beheading of the rebel Scottish Lords on Tower Hill, 1746. They had led the Jacobite rebellion to re-establish a Catholic Stuart monarch on the throne.

ABOVE Friday prayers at the London Central Mosque, Regent's Park, which opened in 1977. The site for the mosque was a gift from the British Government to London's Muslims in 1940.

LEFT A Roman curse, inscribed on lead, laid in a drain at the Roman Amphitheatre under today's Guildhall Yard. It promises a reward to the Goddess Diana for punishing a thief and for the return of the stolen object.

to come. Many, including the giant St Paul's, were destroyed by the Great Fire of 1666.

In London's Christian era, other religions would be discouraged, sometimes suppressed. The invasion of 1066 had brought Jews to London. They settled round what became Old Jewry in the City and in some of the streets close to the Tower. They were mistrusted, often loathed. Rumours of child sacrifice dogged their steps and led to judicial murder and mob revenge. At the coronation of Richard I in 1189 there was a massacre of Jews in London, and in 1290, the Jews were forcibly expelled from England.

Intolerance infected Christianity itself. The Protestant Reformation of the 1530s threw off papal discipline and rejected the trappings of Catholic worship. St Paul's and the other London churches had their altars stripped and their treasures melted down. The Catholic backlash under Queen Mary led to the burning alive of Protestants at Smithfield and Newgate in 1555–57. Gory prints of the London burnings in Foxe's Book of Martyrs would give many a Protestant child nightmares for generations to come. But when Protestantism was re-established under Elizabeth from 1558, the burning of heretics and Catholic recusants in London continued apace.

Internecine religious tensions continued well into the eighteenth century. There were Anglican riots against the Dissenters (Protestants not part of the Church of England) in 1709, sparked off by a turbulent cleric called Sacheverel. The worst troubles, though, concerned the possible return of a Catholic monarch to the English throne. This was not such a far-fetched prospect. In 1715 and again in 1745, invasions took place in the Stuart name and with the genuine prospect of a Catholic revival. The "Forty-Five" brought an army of Highlanders and others as far south as Derby and for a time London was in panic. A bloody revenge saw the traitors' heads taken off on Tower Hill and elsewhere in 1746.

No heads came off in the name of religion in the nineteenth century, but not all was plain sailing. There would be riots in some London churches, even threats to pull churches down, over what many saw as a Catholic takeover by the vestry door. The most dramatic – indeed, farcical – were in the East End in 1859 when hundreds of police were needed at St George's church to stop riots against altar decorations. More important, though, were the unprecedented efforts of evangelicals to reform the poor. The London City Mission sent evangelists into every slum in London from 1835 until the end of the century. Other missions competed for the souls of the poor, prominent among them the Salvation Army, begun in the East End in 1878 by the hellfire preacher "General" William Booth. Much practical work was done to combat ignorance, to aid the sick and help the homeless, especially abandoned and neglected children, the scandal of the age. Thomas Barnardo, whose work began in London around 1867, was a true hero of his times.

Despite these efforts, London remained a Christian city largely in name only. From 1950, as the face of the Londoner began to change through world migration, the city returned to something like the tolerance of Londinium some 1,400 years before. By 2001, the numbers claiming allegiance to other faiths was staggering. Some 640,000 Muslims made up the second largest of all such groups after the Christians. There were 290,000 Hindu worshippers, 150,000 Jews, 104,000 Sikhs, and many others. It was the Temple of Mithras all over again.

JEWISH LONDON

This is a brass hanging lamp from twelfth-century London, probably a Jewish household's "Sabbath lamp". After being expelled from England in 1290, Jews were permitted to return by Oliver Cromwell in the 1650s. Sephardi Jews from Holland, Spain and Portugal clustered in the eastern part of the City and nearby, and during the eighteenth and early nineteenth centuries they were joined by Ashkenazi Jewish communities from Germany and Eastern Europe. The earliest synagogues were in Duke's Place and Bevis Marks, both in the City, but they multiplied beyond number during the mass migration from Eastern Europe in 1881. Most famous of all was the Great Synagogue established in Brick Lane in 1898. It had been built as a Huguenot Church in 1743 and became a Methodist chapel from 1819. Since 1976 it has been the Great London Mosque.

99

Freedom of the Press

WILLIAM Caxton, the father of English printing, was a freeman of the City of London, apprenticed there in the 1430s. He spent much time abroad, and it was while he was in Cologne from around 1470 that he became acquainted with the printing press. Caxton first became a printer and publisher – the two words were interchangeable well into the nineteenth century – in Cologne. In 1475–76 he brought his press to London, setting it up near Westminster Abbey. The first book he published there was probably Chaucer's *The Canterbury Tales*. Caxton died in 1492. His pupil Richard Pynson transferred his press to Fleet Street next year, almost certainly to be near the Inns of Court – the right to print law texts was the most lucrative of the age. In 1500, another Caxton pupil, Wynkyn de Worde, moved there too. The long association of Fleet Street and words had begun.

Books, pamphlets and official proclamations would be the main products of the London press for the next 200 years. The newspaper, designed to give regular "intelligence" through news and advertisements, emerged in the 1690s. The first daily was *The Courant*, begun about 1702. Many of these early papers were of one quarto sheet printed on both sides; few ran to four pages. Hundreds of fly-by-day publications rose up and dropped quickly into the gutter. A few survived. None lasted longer than *The Times*. First begun as *The Daily Universal Register* in 1785, it changed to the snappier title three years later.

News publishing proved problematic in eighteenth-century London. Political instability in the first half of the century restricted the limits of what could safely be said. Criticism of government might be labelled seditious libel, sometimes treason. Publishers, printers and authors faced large fines and life-threatening prison sentences, sometimes worse. Daniel Defoe, the author of *Robinson Crusoe* and a Londoner through and through, was sentenced to stand in the pillory in 1703 for writing a pamphlet satirising the Church of England. His friends kept the missile-throwers at bay. For generations, Parliament was paranoid about its proceedings being publicized in ways it did not control. It did not permit reporting of Parliamentary proceeding, so prosecutions of printers and others remained common into the early 1770s, when Parliamentary reporting became a little easier (though it did not become comprehensive until the early nineteenth century).

The press remained burdened in other ways. Every copy of a newspaper had to pay stamp duty of 4d. That put the price of a daily to 7d, an impossible luxury for a working family. A spirited campaign to publish unstamped newspapers, many of them expressing radical views, emerged in the 1830s. The whole weight of the state was wielded against ragged newsvendors who hawked the unstamped papers in the streets. It all brought these unpopular laws further into disrepute. The stamp duty was cut in 1836 and abolished altogether in 1855. Paper, though, was still subject to duty. That last "tax on knowledge", as it truly was, fell in 1861.

By then, London publishing had already undergone a revolution. The *Illustrated London News*, with its sumptuous woodcuts, brought the forerunner of photojournalism to the London breakfast table from 1842. And *Punch*, the most popular comic paper of the age, first published in July 1841, employed London's most famous artists for its weekly full-page comic cut. Further technological developments in typesetting

ABOVE A page from William Caxton's 1476 edition of Geoffrey Chaucer's *Canterbury Tales*, printed at Westminster. The type was modelled on a contemporary handwriting style.

OPPOSITE Fleet Street, the "Street of Ink" – some called it the Street of Drink – in its bustling heyday in 1961, seen from the *Daily Telegraph* building.

and printing greatly expanded capacity. By 1895, 823 "registered newspapers" of one sort or another were published and printed in London, many from Fleet Street and the surrounding area.

Newspapers remained a vital part of London life throughout the twentieth century. The interwar years in particular saw the spectacular rise of "the Press Baron". In one corner, the Harmsworth Brothers (with Harold becoming Viscount Rothermere). They launched the *Daily Mail* in 1896 and the *Daily Mirror* in 1903, at first just for women readers. In the other corner, Max Aitken, Lord Beaverbrook, who bought the *Daily Express* in 1916. Ever more astonishing incentives were offered to readers in the "circulation wars" of the 1920s and '30s, but from the 1950s things grew quieter. Titles were bought up and merged rather than slogging things out head-to-head. Press Barons did not disappear though: the Australian media entrepreneur Rupert Murdoch bought *The Times* and its stable in 1981.

By the twenty-first century, free speech was pretty much untrammelled in the political arena. Questions of privacy and "fair comment" were more fraught. Falling to the courts to decide, boundaries shifted case by case. That debate, though, had been taken to entirely another league by new inventions: the internet and the worldwide web. *See also facsimile items 18 and 19 in envelope 4, opposite page 92.*

BELOW A printing press on the ice, to the left of the tent, during a Frost Fair in February 1814. The printer is selling souvenirs of the once-in-a-lifetime event.

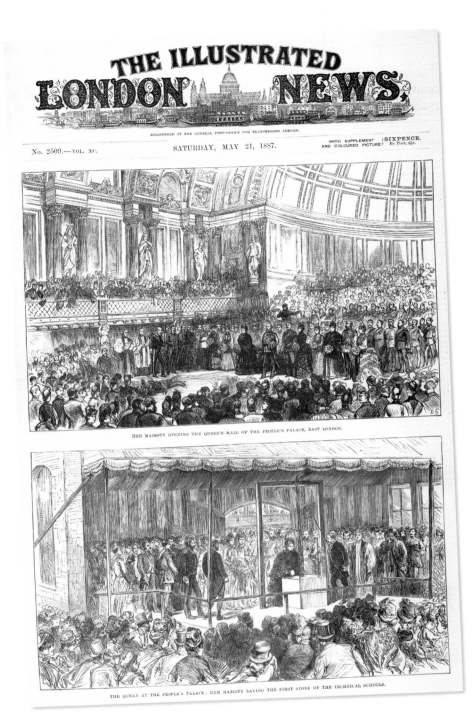

The first book printed in Fleet Street was published by Richard Pynson in 1493 and Wynkyn de Worde set up his printing press there in 1500. Fleet Street and its courts and alleys became associated with newspaper publishing in the eighteenth century and by 1800 at least a dozen were printed there. But it was in the mid-nineteenth century that newspaper production both expanded and clustered ever more densely there, helped by the Press Association's move to Wine Office Court in 1868. By the 1890s it was "Newspaper Land" and home to scores, perhaps hundreds, of titles. So it stayed until the 1980s. The move away from Fleet Street, designed mainly to break the power of the print unions, was engineered by Rupert Murdoch (seen below in his office at Wapping in June 2007), who owned *The Times*, *The Sunday Times*, the *Sun* and the *News of the World*. He shifted production to Wapping after a bloody strike in 1986–87.

ABOVE The *Illustrated London News* of Saturday May 21, 1887, showing the Queen opening The People's Palace, Mile End Road, a centre of workers' education for the East End.

LEFT A late eighteenth-century ticket showing a change of address. There were numerous women printers and publishers in London, often widows who had inherited their husbands' businesses.

103

London, Home of Science

London's love affair with science arrived late in its history. Theoretical and experimental science had been long embedded at Oxford and Cambridge, but it was in London that the first home for British science was established. With encouragement from Charles II, the Royal Society was founded in November 1660 at Gresham College, Bishopsgate, where Sir Christopher Wren was Professor of Astronomy. Its early members included Robert Boyle, who moved from Oxford to Pall Mall in 1668, where he had a back-yard laboratory for his chemical experiments; and Robert Hooke, astronomer and chemist, who took on much of the task of surveying the new London that emerged after the Great Fire. The Royal Society moved to purpose-built premises at Crane Court, Fleet Street, in 1710. It was to be the first of many great London institutions that changed the face of world science.

The Royal Observatory at Greenwich followed closely from 1675. Wren was the architect, and it must have been a labour of love. The second Astronomer Royal there was Edmond Halley, who accurately predicted the next appearance of the comet that would come to bear his name – sixteen years after his death. Time was a necessary obsession of the astronomers, and the Observatory was equipped with two clocks by the famous London clockmaker Thomas Tompion.

It was time and the rotation of the earth that put Greenwich most definitively on the world map. Measurement of longitude was a practical requirement of navigation. In a maritime age it was of both commercial and military significance. John Harrison, a brilliantly innovative clockmaker from Yorkshire, came to London in 1730 to solve the problem. He did so, though for years was treated shabbily by Government for his pains. Eventually, he found the fortune and lasting fame he deserved and the world signed up to Greenwich as the accepted location of the meridian in 1884.

In the nineteenth century, London became a treasure-store of the natural sciences. Its standing was based on collections that went back to the eighteenth century, to the early voyages of discovery and gentleman collectors' magpie enthusiasms. Sir Hans Sloane's collection of everything under the sun was bought for the nation on his death and became an early addition to the British Museum, founded in 1753. But the Museum was not interested in science and the collection was in part sold off and in part fell to dust. Science was rescued from its woeful stewardship by a brand-new Natural History Museum, opened for the nation at South Kensington in 1881. It remains a scientific resource of unique importance.

Other eighteenth-century collections had a happier history. The Royal Botanic Gardens at Kew, as they became in 1841, were based on the plant-collecting passion of the Georgians and began to take something like their modern shape from 1771. They gained enormously from Joseph Paxton's giant greenhouse, the model for his Crystal Palace of 1851. They remain one of the world's great botanic collections, of use to students everywhere. So does the Zoological Society of London's collection at Regent's Park. The Society was formed in 1826, its Zoological Gardens two years later. London Zoo was opened to the public from 1847, one of the city's great attractions, but an important centre for animal research and conservation too.

If theory and discovery remained embedded in the great universities, invention and innovation flourished in London. The radio developed first in London (Marconi had a workshop in Clerkenwell), so did gramophones, and television (John Logie Baird had his laboratory in Soho, and the first TV pictures were beamed from London). London could also claim an honourable role in the development of the computer. The mathematician, economist and inventor Charles Babbage was born in south London in 1791. In 1822 he began work on a "difference engine", a machine to calculate numbers; and later an "analytical engine" based on a system of punch cards. Neither would be made to work in his lifetime, but his ideas were entirely practicable and Babbage remains the father of the machine that changed the world. The Colossus

ABOVE A pocket telescope by John Cuff, one of the foremost scientific instrument-makers of his day, trading at the sign of the Reflecting Microscope and Spectacles, Fleet Street, around 1750.

BELOW Mr Accum, a professor of Chemistry, lecturing to a public audience at the Rotunda or Surrey Institution on the south side of Blackfriars Bridge, 1809.

OVERLEAF The Treetop Walkway at Kew Gardens, opened in May 2008, was mirrored by the underground Rhizotron, affording a worm's-eye view of the trees' rooting systems.

BOTTOM London's medical profession became enormously wealthy during the course of the eighteenth century. The Royal College of Physicians' palatial headquarters in Pall Mall East are pictured here in 1827.

ABOVE The old Royal Observatory, Greenwich, designed by Sir Christopher Wren, 1675. The Prime Meridian of longitude, dividing the eastern and western hemispheres is marked in brass on the cobbles.

computer, used for code-breaking in the Second World War, was developed by Post Office engineers at Dollis Hill, north-west London, in 1943. Post Office Tower staff contributed significantly to the earliest internet networks in 1981. Scientific innovation in London continued to have a number of centres of excellence, none more brilliant than Imperial College, founded in South Kensington in 1907 and a notable world nexus for scientific learning.

A LONDON HISTORY OF TIME

From the second half of the seventeenth century, London led the world in making scientific instruments for measuring space and time, and observing both the universe and the tiniest secrets of nature. Thomas Tompion (c.1639-1713), a blacksmith's son from Bedfordshire, was a clockmaker in London by 1671. Within a few years he had made a watch and clock for Charles II and the most sophisticated clocks of the age for the Tower of London and Royal Observatory. Although his daily business was watchmaking, he also made some of the first mercury barometers and scientific instruments, like this brass Universal Ring Dial of about 1680. It is a navigational aid that can tell the time and calculate the altitude of the sun anywhere in the world except the polar regions. It is astonishingly beautiful too.

Growing Up in London

For centuries the vast majority of children in London grew up less at home or in school than in the streets. There they learned the art of surviving in a great city – of keeping a sharp lookout for all around them, of living by their wits and taking pleasure from the excitement and interest on offer. The street was their playground too, and some toys were made to be specially enjoyed there – hoops, spinning tops, carts of all kinds and bats and balls. More prosperous children, with at least some of the comforts of home life, had toys of greater sophistication like model soldiers and mechanical toys, dolls and dolls' houses.

During much of London's history these enjoyments were short-lived, perhaps not present at all, as children were made into young adults and pressed into the world of work. Spitalfields silk weavers, whose homes were their workshops, expected their children to help wind silk from the age of four or five. Other home trades like matchbox-making, fur-pulling and some tailoring, all depended on child labour. Cruellest of all were the lives of the "climbing boys" sent up chimneys to clean them of soot. They were at risk of suffocation in the crooked narrow chimneys, often still hot, but there were dangers too from soot in the throat and lungs. Many developed "chimney sweep's cancer", of the scrotum.

But for a fortunate minority, London did provide schooling. In medieval London the monks were often teachers. Westminster

LEFT A London chimney sweep in 1861. Around this time the abuses of child labour – some apprentices burnt or suffocated in the flues – were being made illegal.

BELOW LEFT Westminster School in 1890, showing the seventeenth-century Ashburnham House and Inigo Jones's gateway on the right.

BELOW RIGHT A sixteenth-century hornbook for use at home or school. The thin coating of horn, black with age, was originally a protective clear covering for the parchment text below.

RIGHT Many clergymen supplemented their incomes by establishing small boarding schools for the sons of the middle classes. Here is a substantial bill for Master Caldwell's education in 1827, probably at a school in Welling, near Bexleyheath, Kent.

BELOW AND BOTTOM The London education authorities were keen to recognize a pupil's good behaviour at school, awarding medals for attendance, politeness and diligence. Below is a medal awarded by the School Board for London to W. Hampshire in 1901, the last year of Victoria's reign. During the First World War, with metal in short supply, the London County Council replaced medals with elaborate certificates like this one (bottom), for a boy at Townsmead Road Elementary School, Fulham.

School welcomed scholars from 1179, and was probably a monastery school before that. Christ's Hospital (the Bluecoat) School was formed at the dissolution of the monasteries to help make good the loss of monastic teaching. Established by the Bishop of London and rich City merchants, it opened its doors in Newgate Street to poor (but well-connected) children from 1552. And Charterhouse School was founded in 1611 in a former Carthusian monastery near Smithfield. Charterhouse outgrew its ancient site and moved to Surrey in 1872; and Christ's Hospital did the same, transplanting to Sussex in 1902. But Westminster stayed on, and remains at its old home still.

As London grew in size, these venerable institutions became inadequate for Londoners' educational needs. The market could provide tutors and boarding and commercial schools, of sorts, for the middle classes. Often schools would be designed to satisfy parents' religious views; Protestant Dissenters found Hackney especially congenial for schools and seminaries, for instance. But all this did nothing for London's numberless poor.

It was London's parish authorities that began to grapple with this problem from the 1660s. Gradually, and by no means comprehensively, parishes established "charity schools" as a necessary component of religious endeavour. How could people imbibe the Gospel if they could not read the Bible? So reading was the fundamental basis of the charity school initiative. Writing was more of a luxury: imparting it was thought to be tutoring a class above its station. Even so, many went further, into arithmetic and music, and useful trades like needlework. All clothed and fed the children they benefited: both boys and girls were dressed in a charity school uniform. Despite all the reservations modern observers might have, London was vastly proud of its efforts. The Charity Children were paraded in front of doting and tearful London audiences at St Paul's once a year, and at great ceremonials, especially those welcoming foreign dignitaries, they sang their hearts out in choirs some 5,000 strong.

By 1799, there were 207 charity schools in and near London, teaching some 8,000 children. The move to educate the poor gathered fresh momentum from the Sunday School movement around 1785; and from the Ragged Schools that developed in the 1830s and after. These were the first to try to reach the gutter children, the untouchables of London. Heroic efforts were made by the teachers of the Ragged School Union, established in London in 1844, even if learning came with obligatory religious propaganda. Yet it still proved insufficient. In 1870, when compulsory education was at last imposed, nearly 40 per cent of 445,000 school-age children in London were getting no education at all, or something that was "a mere pretence".

So it has only been for the past 140 years that education has entered into the lives of all London's children. And generally that education was of a most elementary kind. Secondary education over the age of 14 did not become established for the majority until after the Second World War. So a truly democratic education system for London has been of very modern invention indeed.

ABOVE Most Londoners had to make their own pleasures with what they found around them. Here is a young explorer on the Thames shore at Tower Beach, 1952.

LEFT Queen Victoria, Prince Albert and their children meet the family of Thomas Younghusband at the Crystal Palace in 1851. The children's rich attire offers a striking contrast to the dress of London's street children of the time.

LEFT Two shoeblacks (shoe-cleaning boys) study the portrait of the Earl of Shaftesbury, a philanthropist who had helped found the London Shoeblack Brigade in 1851. The elder boy wears the Brigade's uniform, in contrast to the ragged urchin at his side.

BELOW Hamleys, London's most famous toyshop, in Regent Street. Founded by William Hamley in Holborn in 1760, a Regent Street branch was first opened in 1881.

LONDON'S LITTLE ADULTS

Until the early eighteenth century, girls and boys were dressed like miniature versions of their parents. This portrait of Henry Frederick, Prince of Wales, from around 1604 (when he was just 10 years old) shows him in the sort of silver slashed doublet and lace collar that his father, James I, would have worn. But a move to informality in children's clothes, and the dressiness which Spitalfields silks made possible relatively cheaply, began a trend to dress children distinctively in clothes made especially for them. Among the poor, though, the tradition of children using cast-offs and cut-down adult clothing – sometimes entirely unsuitably – continued well into the early twentieth century, as the picture of the "young hooligan" on p.114 eloquently shows.

London's Underworld

There is an extraordinary continuity in London's criminal past. The crimes that plagued it for centuries were there from the very beginning. The classic London crime was cheating – frauds, confidence tricks, sleight of hand, forgery and counterfeit coining. The earliest printed guides to London warned against the tricks of the town to be met with in streets and taverns. Second to the London sharper came the light-fingered pickpocket, a problem from time immemorial. Moll Cutpurse, a popular nickname for a woman pickpocket, was common currency in seventeenth-century London and doubtless before. In the eighteenth century she would be called Jenny Diver. The shoplifter, the housebreaker, and the burglar with nerves of steel who broke into occupied houses at night, plagued both middle-class householders and the poor who might have a little something to steal.

Street robbers – "muggers" later ages would call them – were legion, their weapons a bludgeon or a knife, sometimes a pistol. They were considered low-class bullies. Highwaymen were more noteworthy, even more respectable. They robbed on horseback, generally at night, their cry "Stand and Deliver!", their stock armaments a brace of flintlock pistols. They were famously gallant to ladies. The highwayman Dick Turpin, born in Essex around 1705, has also entered legend. He was especially active on the commons and heaths around London from 1734; after his celebrated ride on Black Bess, he was hanged at York in 1739.

Legendary London villains emerged in modern times too. The East End gang of Ronnie and Reggie Kray, twins born in Hoxton in 1933, extracted protection money from nightclubs and casinos with stop-at-

nothing violence. Though their murder victims were all underworld types, the killings underlined the twins' ruthlessness to all who had dealings with them. The Krays' glitzy lifestyle and charitable giving – they had a particular attraction for showbiz personalities – made them celebrities in Swinging London. All that stopped with their imprisonment for life in March 1969. Their demise did not bring London gangland to an end, but no subsequent villains impacted on metropolitan life in quite the way the Krays had done.

FINDING THE MUTILATED BODY IN MITRE SQARE

JACK SHEPPARD

Jack Sheppard was a legend in his own lifetime and for long after. Born in Spitalfields in 1702, Jack was apprenticed to his father's trade as a carpenter, where he discovered how locks and buildings worked. This stood him in good stead when he later became a thief and burglar. But it was his extraordinary skill as a prison-breaker that stunned contemporaries and made his name live on. He escaped first from the round-house or local lock-up of St Giles-in-the-Fields, then made a remarkable exit from the New Prison in Clerkenwell. Most spectacular of all were his two escapes from Newgate, the first just four days before he was due to be executed. His last escape saw him free himself from handcuffs and great iron fetters, take an iron bar from the chimney, climb up, break through the wall into the room above his cell, and open six locked and bolted doors until he found himself on the roof of the gaol. He let himself down from the roof, broke silently into a neighbouring house and made his escape into the street. All London was agog. But he was captured once more, watched round the clock, and eventually hanged, aged just 22, at Tyburn on November 16, 1724.

Murder, they say, will out. And London's long history has been punctuated by some horrific crimes. Often the perpetrator walked free, because no age had yet perfected the art of detection. Some of the crimes were so horrific that they resonated for generations.

The great murder sensation of the nineteenth century was Jack the Ripper, the first sexual serial killer of international importance. In the East End of London, in the autumn of 1888, Jack the Ripper committed at least five murders, all of prostitutes. There is dispute about the precise number but all "Ripperologists" agree on at least five murders: Mary Anne (Polly) Nichols, in Buck's Row, Whitechapel, on August 31; Annie Chapman in a back yard at Hanbury Street, Spitalfields, on September 8; Long Liz Stride, at Berner Street, Stepney, and Catherine Eddowes, at Mitre Square, City, on September 30; and, most horrific and crazed of all, Mary Jane Kelly at her room in Miller's Court, Dorset Street on November 9. Over 130 suspects have been named as the killer, and the list will probably grow longer. Despite the fanciful attributions, from members of the Royal Family to eminent artists, the killer was never likely to be identified.

Perhaps the most significant murderer of twentieth-century London was John Reginald Halliday Christie. Born in Yorkshire in 1899, Christie moved to London in 1923. In 1938, he rented 10 Rillington Place, a slum property in Notting Dale. In 1949, he murdered the wife and baby of his tenant, Timothy Evans. Evans was hanged for the murder of his baby that same year. When Christie left Rillington Place in 1953, the truth finally came out. The new occupier discovered the remains of women whom Christie had murdered from his time as a special constable in the Blitz and after: Ruth Fuerst (1943), Muriel Eady (1944), his wife Ethel (about 1948) and three prostitutes. Most had been sexually assaulted at the time of, or after, their murders.

The miscarriage of justice in the Evans case resonated in the British judicial system: the last hanging in Britain would take place in 1964.

ABOVE A young "hooligan", around 1900. The word apparently gained popularity in the 1890s through a South London family of that name, notorious for thieving and violence.

LEFT Ronnie and Reggie Kray with their mother Violet and grandfather Jimmy, in 1965. Although strong on family values, they were the most notorious gangsters of their age.

OPPOSITE John Reginald Halliday Christie in a "black Maria" police van in April 1953, having been charged with the murder of six women at 10 Rillington Place, Notting Dale.

Police, Prisons and Punishments

FOR centuries there was no London-wide policing at all. Householders would meet once a year to elect a constable to make arrests, charge prisoners and hire men to "watch" their local streets nightly and cry the hours and state of the weather to the inhabitants. Night-watchmen sheltered from the rain in watch-boxes and managed the parish lock-up or "round-house". The watchmen, popularly known as "Charlies", were often decrepit elderly paupers, whose labour was cheap but who were far from active. Tormenting the Charlies became a popular pastime of young men about town.

As the wealthy part of London's population grew, and shops and houses had more valuables in them than ever before, the ravages of thieves and street-robbers became less and less tolerable. People went armed with swords in the streets, and with pistols and blunderbusses in their carriages. And from time to time, the night watch was supplemented by a Horse Patrol around the edge of London to deter highwaymen. But there were no police who would investigate a crime once committed, or be able to recover stolen property, until the 1750s. Then, the first detective police force was established by Henry Fielding, the playwright and novelist, who was senior magistrate at

OPPOSITE Executions were held in public until 1868, at first at Tyburn as shown here, and from 1783 outside Newgate. Scenes of chaos, drunkenness and violence often ensued.

BELOW Night watchmen were often subject to attack. This 1820 Cruickshank engraving is entitled "Tom Getting the Best of a Charley", using the popular slang term of the day.

Bow Street, London's main court outside the City. These men would become the famous "Bow Street Runners". There were only six of them at the start, but they became renowned experts in London's villains and their haunts. They were even hired to catch thieves by rich householders who had suffered robberies elsewhere in England.

The problem of preventing crime, apart from the nightly watch, remained untouched until 1829 when Home Secretary Sir Robert Peel established a London-wide police force. The Metropolitan Police Force, with uniformed men (and from the First World War, women too) patrolled the streets by day as well as night. Their district was the whole of built-up London and the villages beyond. For the first time, the streets of London were put on something like an orderly and safe footing.

Once criminals were arrested and convicted they had to be locked up. London was a city of prisons – there were no fewer than 19 there in 1800 – and the greatest of all was the Tower of London. The Tower was where major offenders against the king or religious

authority were detained and punished. Some of the most famous Britons were imprisoned here for a time, even kings and queens, princes and princesses. The prisoners included Sir Thomas More, Sir Walter Raleigh, Guy Fawkes, and Lord George Gordon, architect of the terrible riots of 1780.

Next in importance to the Tower was Newgate Prison, London's main gaol for over 800 years. At least two of the gates in the Roman walls of London – Newgate and Ludgate – had been prisons from medieval times at least. After the Great Fire of 1666, the prisons and courthouses were the first public buildings to be rebuilt. Newgate was extended and rebuilt again in the 1770s to a design of George Dance the Younger. It was the central prison for those on remand for major crimes, for City debtors and for prisoners awaiting execution and transportation. It did not finally close until the turn of the twentieth century.

Traitors were publicly beheaded on Tower Hill up to the middle of the eighteenth century. But ordinary criminals were hanged (and

heretics or women guilty of treason were sometimes burned) at Smithfield until the sixteenth century, and then generally at Tyburn, roughly where Marble Arch now stands. Public executions moved outside Newgate from 1783, where most of London's hangings took place. The last (of an Irish terrorist) was in 1868. From then until 1964, executions would be private affairs behind prison walls. Executions were not the only means of public punishment. Some prisoners were whipped through the streets at the cart's tail; others were branded or humiliated in the pillory. These old punishments were not finally abandoned in London until the 1830s.

The London prison system was drastically overhauled in the nineteenth century. The ancient gaols – including the notorious debtors' prisons at the Fleet, the Marshalsea and the King's Bench – were demolished and built over for housing. By 1901, there were just five London prisons, all planted in the suburbs of the time – Brixton, Pentonville, Wandsworth, Holloway and Wormwood Scrubs. The last was built by convict labour.

A century on and these places had become old and tired in their turn. It looked as though they might well share the fate of their forbears: to be demolished, and replaced by London's insatiable demand for modern housing.

See also facsimile item 20 in envelope 4, opposite page 92.

ABOVE "Night Charges on Their Way to the Court", an engraving from *The Graphic*, December 1869, showing uniformed police officers with drunks and thieves.

BELOW A view of one of the interior courtyards at Newgate Prison, London's main jail for over 800 years, until its closure in 1902 and demolition two years later. The Old Bailey now stands on the site.

ABOVE The Tower of London has stood by the Thames for over 900 years. The Traitor's Gate, which opens on to the river, allowed prisoners to be brought in by boat; many never left the Tower again. Executions, such as those of Anne Boleyn and Lady Jane Grey, took place within the grounds of the Tower.

LEFT A modern Metropolitan Police helmet badge. London's police force is one of the oldest in the country, first taking to the streets on September 29, 1829.

INDEX

Page numbers in **bold** indicate pictures/captions. Memorabilia in envelopes are indexed as E and then the item number; images on the envelopes are **bold** and facsimiles are *italics*.

FURTHER READING

Hebbert, Michael *London. More by Fortune than Design*, Wiley, 1998

Hibbert, Christopher, Ben Weinreb et al *The London Encyclopaedia*, Macmillan, 2008

Inwood, Stephen *A History of London*, Macmillan, 1998

Inwood, Stephen *Historic London: An Explorer's Companion*, Macmillan, 2008

Porter, Roy *London. A Social History*, Penguin, 2000

Sheppard, Francis *London: A History*, Oxford University Press, 1998

White, Jerry *London in the Twentieth Century. A City and Its People*, Vintage, 2008

White, Jerry *London in the Nineteenth Century. 'A Human Awful Wonder of God'*, Vintage, 2008

ACKNOWLEDGEMENTS

More than most books, this has been very much a collaborative venture. The idea originated with Penny Craig at Carlton Publishing Ltd, whose energy, efficiency and good humour have brought the project to a successful conclusion within a very short timescale. She has been ably assisted by Lucy Coley and Rachel Burgess. The staff of the Museum of London have responded generously to the various challenges of identifying, collating and reproducing material for the illustrations and facsimiles, despite competing demands of great significance for the Museum's future. Many have been involved in this project and I thank them all; but I would like particularly to mention the invaluable roles played by David Spence, Beverley Cook, John Clark and Sean Waterman. Finally, my special thanks go to Rosie Cooper, who has had to live with my London obsession for over twenty years and who has given me unflagging, if bemused, support. Without it none of this would have been possible.

ABOVE A sign like this would have been put in the doorway or foyer of a 1930s' London cinema to keep the waiting audience in line.

PICTURE CREDITS

Key: t = top, b = bottom, l = left, r = right and c = centre.

IMAGES SUPPLIED BY THE MUSEUM OF LONDON
(Artist/creator and date are given in brackets after the page reference)

Museum of London: front endpaper, 1, 3, 4, 5, 9t, 9b, 10-11, 14, 15, 16 (Joseph Van Aken, 1726–30), 17t (London County Council, 1920), 17b (F. Berry, 1882), 18bl, 18-19, 19br (Henry Flather, 1866–68), 20 (Mick Buxton of Valhalla Models), 22 (Robert Dighton, 1807), 23 (Gustave Doré, 1872), 24tl, 24tr, 24br (John Thomson, c.1877), 25br (John Chase), 26tr, 27tl, 27c, 27bc, 27br (Hablot Knight Browne, c.1839), 28t (George Harcourt Sephton, 1859), 28b, 29tl, 29tr, 30–31 (Dirck Roderigo Stoop, 1662), 32 (George Scharf, 1829), 33bl (Alfred Pearse, c.1910), 33br (Giovanni Battista Cipriani, Sir Robert Taylor, 1757), 34-35, 35r, 36 (George Scharf, 1818), 37t (Francis Wheatley, James Heath, 1790), 37bl, 37br, 38l, 42, 43tl, 43b, 44, 45b (Abraham Hondius, 1684), 46b (John Thomson, c.1878), 48 (Thomas Rowlandson [engraver], J.C. Stadler [aquatinter], 1808), 49bl, 50-51 (Philippe-Jacques de Loutherbourg [artist], John Chapman [artist publisher], F. Bartolozzi [engraver], 1778), 52t (Thomas Rowlandson, H. Merke, 1799), 52b (Rudulph Ackerman, 1809), 53 (T.M Baynes, W.Duryer, 1823), 55t, 55cr, 55br, 56-57, 58tl, 58br, 59tl, 59c (J. Tarts, c.1770), 59br, 60bl (John Thomson, c.1877), 60tr, 61 (Charles Booth, 1889), 62 (Thomas Rowlandson [artist], A.C. Pugin [engraver], Sunderland [aquatinter], 1809), 63b, 64 (Samuel Wale [artist], I. S. Muller [engraver], 1750), 65t (Joseph Nash, 1852), 65br, 66-67 (John Ritchie, 1858), 68-69, 70 (William Hogarth, c.1773), 71t (Thomas Rowlandson [artist], Augustus Charles Pugin [engraver], 1808), 72-73, 73cr, 73br, 74t, 74b, 75, 77tr, 77br, 80 (Alice Havers, 1886), 81bl (John & Thomas Bowles, 1748), 81br, 82bl, 82br, 84t, 84-85 (Louise Rayner, 1870), 86-87, 88 (Thomas Rowlandson, 1810–15), 89tl, 90t, 90b (John Dunstall, 1666), 91t (John Thomson, c.1877), 91b, 92 (William Hogarth, 1735), 93tl (Augustus Charles Pugin, Thomas Rowlandson, 1808), 93tr, 94-95 (John O'Connor, 1874), 95r (Benson's Advertising Agency, 1921–30), 96, 96-97 (Robert Wilkinson,1746), 98t (John Chase, 1993), 98b, 99br, 100 (William Caxton, 1476), 102, 103t, 103bl, 105tr, 105cr (Thomas Rowlandson, 1809), 105br (Thomas Hosmer Shepherd, 1827), 107br (Thomas Tompion, 1666–1700), 108c (Henry Mayhew, 1861), 108bl (F.P. Barraud [artist], F. Hunter [etcher], 1890), 108br, 109cl, 109tr, 109b, 110b (C. Wells, c.1854), 111t (William MacDuff, 1862), 111br (Robert Peake – The Elder, 1603-1605), 112t (R. Cooper [engraver], 1815-1820), 112b, 113br (James Thornhill, 1724), 114t, 116 (George Cruikshank, I. Robert Cruikshank, 1820), 117 (William Hogarth, 1747), 118t, 118b. Envelope 1: outside envelope (Gustave Doré, 1882); item 1 (Georg Braun, Frans Hogenberg, 1574); item 2; item 3 (London County Council). Envelope 2: outside envelope; item 4 (Woolworth's); item 5; item 6; item 7; item 8. Envelope 3: outside envelope (Abram Games, 1951); item 9; item 10; item 11; item 12; item 13. Envelope 4: outside envelope; item 14; item 15; item 16; item 18; item 19; item 20, back endpaper (Thomas Luny, 1835).

Bank of England/Museum of London, reproduced under the terms of the Click-Use Licence: item 17 (in Envelope 3).

City of London Police/Museum of London, reproduced by kind permission of the Commissioner of the City of London Police: 40-41 (Arthur Cross, Fred Tibbs, 1941)

Peter Froste/Museum of London: 8 (Peter Froste)

Ian Galt/Museum of London: 99l (John Galt. c.1900),

Henry Grant Collection/Museum of London: 38-39 (Henry Grant, 1978), 54 (Henry Grant, c.1952), 89tr (Henry Grant, 1955), 93b (Henry Grant, 1956), 110t (Henry Grant, 1952)

PLA Collection/Museum of London: 45t, 46t

IMAGES FROM OTHER SUPPLIERS:

Corbis: 21, 29b

Condé Nast Archive: 83tr

Getty Images: 27bl, 33t, 76, 89b, 103br, 106-107, 118t, 119b; /AFP: 49tl; /Mark Allan: 83b; /John Lamb: 47; /Adrian Lyon: 71b; /National Geographic: 101; /Wireimage.com: 83t

Hulton-Deutsch Collection: 114b; /Michael Nicholson: 49br; /Andy Rain/EPA: 77bc

Istockphoto.com: 6-7

NHS: 91b

Rex Features: 63t, 78-79; /Nicholas Bailey: 111bl; / Nils Jorgensen: 55bc; /David Pearson: 59bl; /Alex Segre: 25; /Yannick Yanoff: 12-13

Topfoto.co.uk: 26tl, 104-105, 113l